Falls in Older Persons

Prevention and Management

second edition

Falls in Older Persons

Prevention and Management

second edition

Rein Tideiksaar, Ph.D.

Baltimore • London • Winnipeg • Sydney

Health Professions Press, Inc.
Post Office Box 10624
Baltimore, Maryland 21285-0624

Typeset by PRO-IMAGE Corporation, York, Pennsylvania.
Manufactured in the United States of America by
Versa Press, Inc., East Peoria, Illinois.

Cover design by Four Winds Productions, LLC, Baltimore, Maryland.
Illustrations by Juanita Wassenaar-Beggs.

Library of Congress Cataloging-in-Publication Data

Tideiksaar, Rein.
Falls in older persons : prevention and management / Rein Tideiksaar. — 2nd ed.
p. cm.
Includes bibliographical references and index.
ISBN 1-878812-44-0
1. Falls (Accidents) in old age. 2. Falls (Accidents) in old age—Prevention. 3. Aged—Hospital care. 4. Aged—Nursing home care. I. Title.
RC952.5.T53 1998
617.1′0084′6—dc21 98-5138
CIP

British Library Cataloguing in Publication Data are available from the British Library.

Contents

About the Author

Rein Tideiksaar, Ph.D., is Director of Clinical and Educational Programs, Department of Geriatrics, Southwest Medical Associates, Sierra Health Services, Inc., Las Vegas, and clinical faculty member at the University of Nevada School of Medicine. Prior to 1996 he was a faculty member at the Henry L. Schwartz Department of Geriatrics, Mount Sinai Medical Center, New York, and Director of its Falls and Immobility Program.

He obtained a Ph.D. from Columbia Pacific University and a P.A. from the State University of New York at Stony Brook. Dr. Tideiksaar completed his geriatric training at the Parker Jewish Geriatric Institute, New York.

Dr. Tideiksaar has written numerous articles, book chapters, and the textbook, *Falling in Old Age: Prevention and Management*, on the topic of falls in older adults, conducted fall-related research, and has developed fall-prevention programs in both acute care hospital and nursing facility settings. He also directs a falls consultative service in a managed care facility.

Preface

The first edition of this book (then entitled *Falls in Older Persons: Prevention and Management in Hospitals and Nursing Homes*) was published in 1993. The goals of that edition were quite simple: first, to provide institutionally based health care professionals with an introduction to the topic of falls and an understanding of their extent, consequences, and the numerous factors involved in causing falls; second, to provide a practical and organized approach to preventing and managing falls; and third, to provide a bibliography that addresses specifically the problem of falls and fall-prevention programs in hospitals and nursing facilities, thus allowing the reader to explore the field in more depth. The enthusiastic response to that book and the many suggestions I received from readers encouraged me to undertake a second edition.

The reasons and circumstances that prompted the first edition continue to exist. The number of older adults who use acute care hospital and long-term care facility services is increasing steadily. Because of the deteriorating effects of acute and chronic illness and functional disability, older people are most vulnerable to the problem of falls and their related complications. Their vulnerability has created a demand for fall-prevention efforts.

The second edition updates the chapters, reflecting the many developments in the field since 1993. The bibliography also has been updated to reflect new writings and research. As in the first edition, the subject of mechanical restraints is addressed. Although not the primary focus of this book, I felt it necessary to include a separate chapter and extensive bibliography on mechanical and chemical restraints because falls occurring in hospitals and nursing facilities are a leading reason for their use. More important, as we are beginning to understand, mechanical and chemical restraints are more harmful than beneficial in the prevention of falls and the management of fall risk.

It is my hope that readers find this edition as valuable as the first and that they either adapt key elements of this book into existing fall-prevention programs for improvements or design a program from the beginning.

...

Handout materials that are ready for photoduplication can be found throughout the book (handouts are identified by the copyright line at the bottom of the form). Permission from Health Professions Press to use these materials for in-service or educational workshops is not necessary. Materials are not intended for promotional or commercial purposes and should not be used in either way without obtaining permission from the publisher.

Introduction

One of the most common and often critical problems faced by institutionally based health care providers is that of falls among older adults. Hospital falls represent a leading cause of adverse events, accounting for 25%–89% of all reported inpatient incidents.[1,2] To a large extent, this wide range is attributable to differences in various institutional policies (i.e., how falls are defined and reported) and the specific site or location of fall occurrence (e.g., rehabilitation, psychiatric, critical care, orthopedics, medical, surgical). Regardless, people age 65 and older experience the majority of these falls. Studies that compare the age distribution of people with falls show that older people are overrepresented,[3,4] averaging about 1.5 falls per bed annually.[5] As many as 50% of these older inpatients fall repeatedly.[6,7] In the nursing facility, a setting older people are admitted to often for safety reasons, falling is equally problematic. More than 50% of all nursing

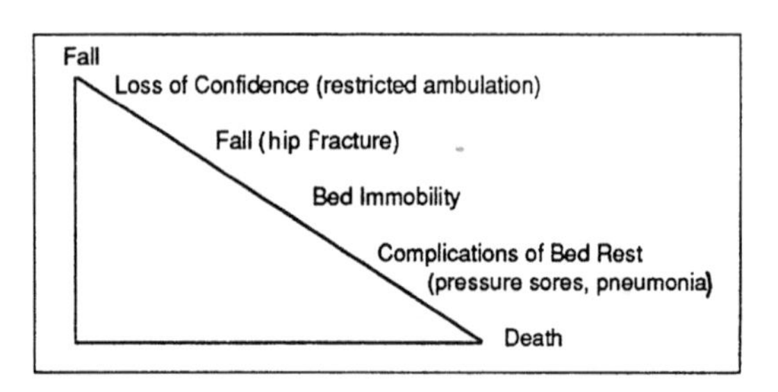

The downward-spiraling effects of falls.

facility residents fall each year, and greater than 40% experience recurrent episodes.[8,9] The probability of falling, in both hospitals and nursing facilities, increases with advancing age; the highest incidence of falling occurs in the 80- to 89-year-old age group.[10,11] This high incidence is more a reflection of the increasing illness and frailty that accompanies aging than it is of old age itself. Falls, particularly repeated falls, are a major cause of physical and psychological trauma. Falls that occur repeatedly are likely to produce a cumulative adverse effect on the individual's capacity for mobility, causing periods of immobility and, as an outcome of complications, premature death (see the illustration above).

In an effort to prevent falls, health care professionals have tried to protect patients and residents by limiting their mobility, often resorting to the use of mechanical or chemical restraints. However, mobility restrictions and restraint use have proven to be ineffective in reducing falls and are associated with a host of negative outcomes for older people. Moreover, federal and state governing bodies responsible for regulating hospitals and nursing facilities have focused their attention during the 1990s on the problem of mechanical and chemical restraints and the methods employed to reduce them. In particular, they have stated strongly that mechanical restraints have a very limited role in the prevention of falls and are asking institutions to implement restraint-reduction programs. A better understanding of the phenomenon of falls will help health care professionals to prevent falls without resorting to traditional methods.

Historically, the blame for falling has, for the most part, been borne by the host, the person who falls. Popular mythology holds that falls are attributable to either individual carelessness or the process of aging. Falls are considered to be either a "normal" phenomenon of aging—a manifestation of a general decline bound to occur—or, in people with multiple disorders, one aspect of a "hopeless" state in which one disorder after another leads inevitably to a negative conclusion. Many health care providers have dealt with falls and their adverse consequences for so long that they have become hardened; they no longer identify them as problems with solutions, other than to restrict the individuals' mobility. Moreover, providers may be reluctant to expect the possibility of better solutions.

Contrary to popular myth, falls, to a large degree, rarely "just happen"—they are neither accidental nor random events—but are predictable occurrences, the outcome of a multitude of host-related and environmental factors that occur either alone or in conjunction with one another. Many of the factors that contribute to falls are potentially amenable to interventions. By minimizing or eliminating these risk factors, falls can be reduced or prevented altogether.

In order to implement preventive measures, health care providers must take the following steps. First, they must understand the conditions under which falls occur and the factors that are associated with fall risk. With an increased knowledge of why older people fall and what factors are associated with fall risk, providers are able to more easily identify patients and residents at risk and explore appropriate solutions aimed at reducing fall risk. Many of the factors responsible for falls are quite easy to fix, particularly for someone with a practiced eye, a different perspective, and different expertise. The second step health care providers must take is to mount an organized approach to the clinical assessment of fall risk and falls and put in place intervention strategies for both.

Chapter 1 examines the outcome of falls with respect to their consequences in patients and residents, their families, and the institution. Chapter 2 reviews the multiple age-related physiological changes, pathological conditions, medications, and environmental and institutional factors associated with falls and fall risk. The clinical approach to the assessment of both falls and fall risk is examined in Chapter 3. Chapter 4 explores a number of medical, rehabilitative, and environmental strategies that reduce fall risk. Common environmental causes of falling (e.g., the condition of lighting, ground surfaces, furnishings) and their modifications are covered in Chapter 5. Chapter 6 is devoted to a discussion of the issues surrounding mechanical and chemical restraints in the management of falls.

Although hospitals and nursing facilities more or less differ in their goals, distribution and orientation of staff, population of individuals cared for, and environmental design principles (see the table below), the factors associated with falls as well as intervention strategies within each institution are similar. However, when it becomes necessary to consider the specificity of each institution, it is noted and differences appropriate to each are set forth.

...

Falls are complex problems, often associated with a variety of causes. A great deal is known about older adults and falls—a wealth of information on their causes, and more important, on how to prevent falls is available. The challenge is how to take what is known and apply it. Although there is no "quick fix" for preventing falls, evidence suggests that an organized approach toward identifying patients and residents at risk for falling and targeting interventions aimed at reducing risk is beneficial. To achieve this goal, health care professionals in hospitals and nursing facilities need to make a long-term commitment to seriously addressing the problem of falls as they apply to their individ-

Characteristics of hospitals and nursing facilities

	Hospital	Nursing facility
Goal	Diagnose and treat acute disease	Manage chronic disease; maintain physical and cognitive function
Population	Patients are medically unstable (acute illness and/or exacerbations of chronic disease); institutional stay temporary	Residents are medically stable but require ongoing medical or personal assistance; in general, institutional stay is long term
Staff	Acute care orientation Daily physician presence Increased nursing staff:patient ratio	Chronic care orientation Irregular physician presence Decreased nursing staff:patient ratio
Environment	Designed to facilitate acute medical care services	Designed to accommodate residents' level of function

ualized setting by developing clinical programs focused on preventing falls.

NOTES

[1]Jones, W.A., & Smith, A. (1989). Preventing hospital incidents: What we can do. *Nursing Management*, 20, 58–60.

[2]Maciorowiski, L.F., Bruno, B., Dietrick-Gallagher, M., McNew, C., Sheppard-Hinkel, E., Wanich, C., & Regan, P. (1988). A review of the patient fall literature. *Journal of Nursing Quality Assurance*, 3, 18–27.

[3]Goodwin, M.B., & Westbrook, J.I. (1993). An analysis of patient accidents in hospital. *Australian Clinical Review*, 13(3),141–149.

[4]Raz, T., & Baretich, M.F. (1987). Factors affecting the incidence of patient falls in hospital. *Medical Care*, 25, 185–195.

[5]Rubenstein, L.Z., Robbins, A.S., Schulman, B.L., Rosado, J., Osterweil, D., & Josephson, K.R. (1988). Falls and instability in the elderly. *Journal of the American Geriatrics Society*, 36, 278–288.

[6]Caley, L.M., & Pinchoff, D.M. (1994). A comparison study of patient falls in a psychiatric setting. *Hospital and Community Psychiatry*, 45, 823–825.

[7]Gaebler, S. (1993). Predicting which patient will fall...and again. *Journal of Advanced Nursing*, 18, 1895–1902.

[8]Clark, R.D., Lord, S.R., & Webster, I.W. (1993). Clinical parameters associated with falls in an elderly population. *Gerontology*, 39, 117–123.

[9]Gurwitz, J.H., Sanchez-Cross, M.T., Eckler, M.A., & Matulis, J. (1994). The epidemiology of adverse events in the long-term care setting. *Journal of the American Geriatrics Society*, 42, 33–38.

[10]Luukinen, H., Koski, L., Hiltunen, L., & Kivela, S.L. (1994). Incidence rate of falls in an aged population in northern Finland. *Journal of Clinical Epidemiology*, 47, 843–850.

[11]Rubenstein, L.Z., Robbins, A.S., Josephson, K.R., Schulman, B.L., & Osterweil, D. (1990). The value of assessing falls in an elderly population: A randomized clinical trial. *Annals of Internal Medicine*, 113, 308–316.

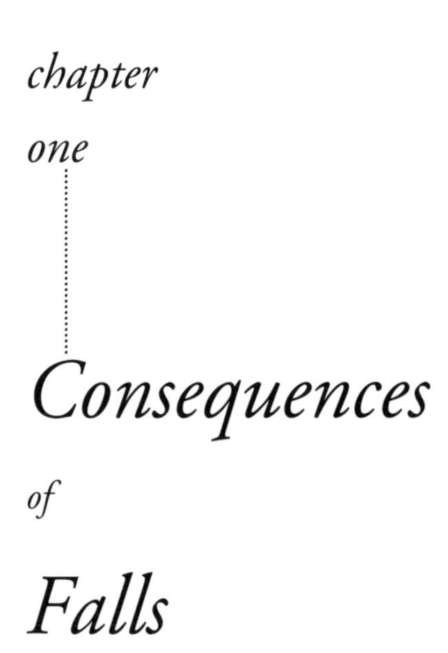

Falls represent a major source of death and disability in older people and pose a serious threat to their health and well-being. The consequences of falls are not confined to older people. They place a burden on family members, make excessive demands on health care professionals, and strain the resources of institutions.

Mortality

Falls and their consequences are a leading cause of death in people 65 years old and older.[1] About 10,000 older adults die each year as a result of falls.[2,3] The risk of dying from a fall increases as people age. Fall-related death rates among people 65 years old and older are 10–150 times higher than those in younger age groups. Of all deaths due to falls, 66% involve people age 75 or older; they have a mortality

Terminology

Clustering of falls	Multiple falling events occurring over a short period of time
Colles fracture	Distal forearm fracture (or fracture of the wrist)
Comorbidity	Presence of additional diseases or illnesses
Contractions (of joints)	Shortening or tightening of a muscle that causes decreased joint motion
Femoral neck	Head of the long bone of the thigh
Orthostatic hypotension	Lowered blood pressure that occurs on rising to an erect position
Osteoporosis	Decrease in bone strength

rate eight times higher than that for individuals from 65 to 74 years of age.[3] More than two thirds of injury-reported deaths after age 85 are related to falls.[4] Of those individuals admitted to the hospital after a fall, only about 50% will be alive 1 year later. Within the hospital setting, about 10% of older patients who have fallen die before discharge. In nursing facilities approximately 1,800 fatal falls occur annually.[4] For people age 85 and older, it is estimated that one in every five falls results in death.[5] A clustering of falls is associated with increased mortality.[6]

Fall-related mortality appears to be the direct result of the fall (e.g., injuries sustained) and current comorbidity (e.g., pneumonia, heart failure, pulmonary disease). Older people have decreased body reserves, and, once injured following a fall, they have a much higher likelihood of dying than do younger people. The use of mechanical restraints to guard against the risk of falls also has been implicated as a cause of death. Most commonly, with the restraint device in place, a person falls or climbs out of bed, slides off a chair, or slips downward in a raised hospital bed. They become entangled and suspended in the restraint—usually pressed tightly against their chest or throat—and die from asphyxia.[7]

Protective reflex	Extension of the arms outward and/or a shift of the feet to maintain balance and avoid a fall
Pulmonary embolism	Blockage of pulmonary artery or one of its branches
Soft-tissue injury	For example, sprains and strains
Subdural hematoma	Accumulation of blood resulting from injury to the brain
Venous stasis	Blood trapped in an extremity (e.g., arm, leg) by compression of veins
Vestibular dysfunction	Impaired vestibular function
Vestibular function	Mechanism within the inner ear involved in balance control

MORBIDITY

The consequences of falls are numerous, from physical injury to immobility to psychosocial trauma to a morbid fear of falling again.

Physical Injury

Half of all hospitalizations resulting from injurious falls are experienced by people in the over-65 age group, and people hospitalized for fall-related trauma are discharged to nursing facilities more often than are individuals without falls. Within the institutional setting, an estimated 16% of falls occurring to older people result in physical injury, approximately 4% result in fractures, and around 12% result in other serious injuries such as head injuries, soft-tissue injuries, musculoskeletal sprains, and lacerations.[5] The most common fractures are those of the distal forearm and hip. Distal forearm, or Colles, fractures occur when an older person loses balance and attempts to break a fall in progress by extending the arms outward. After age 70, there is a decrease in the incidence of forearm fractures, at which time there is a steep increase in the incidence of hip fractures and head injuries. A diminished ability of the older person to exhibit the protective reflex is usually given as the cause of the decline in distal forearm fractures.

It has been hypothesized that a decline in the protective reflex may be attributed to age-related changes in central nervous system function (e.g., decreased reaction and response times), concomitant diseases (e.g., stroke, Parkinson's disease, arthritis), and certain drugs (e.g., psychotropics, hypnotics).[14] Consequently, older people who fall are at great risk for head trauma as well as hip fracture.

Falls are a leading cause of head injury in older people. Aside from bruises and lacerations, the most important head injury is that of subdural hematoma, which tends to occur more frequently than other injuries because of certain age-related changes in the older brain such as decreased cerebral reserve. As a result, older people are less able than younger people to withstand even minor trauma such as might occur from bumping a wall, a bed side rail, or a headboard. Any time a person sustains mental confusion following a fall, a subdural hematoma should be suspected and then ruled out by a neurological evaluation. Any lingering subdural hematoma that has not healed within a relatively short period of time can lead to permanent cognitive dysfunction.

Approximately 2.9% of falls result in hip fracture.[8] Although the incidence of hip fractures is low, the subsequent mortality and morbidity is substantial. Of all hip fracture patients 4% die in the hospital,[9] and within 1 year after their injury up to 23% are dead;[10] people 75 years old and older have the highest mortality rates.[1] A high incidence of coexisting chronic diseases in people with hip fracture contributes to this increased mortality rate. After a hip fracture many older people never regain their premorbid level of ambulation. Approximately 60% of people have decreased mobility; another 25% become functionally dependent in walking and require mechanical assistance (e.g., the use of a cane or walker) or the assistance of another person.[1] Of all hip fracture survivors 14% remain in the nursing facility 1 year after injury.[11]

The risk of sustaining a hip fracture from a fall is dependent on a number of interacting factors, including the height of the fall and impact surface, protective reflexes, "shock absorbers," and bone strength.

Height of the Fall and Impact Surface

In order to build sufficient momentum to produce injury (e.g., bone fracture), an individual must fall a considerable distance. For example, an unexpected fall from a standing height (e.g., a slip, loss of consciousness) or a fall from an elevated bed height (e.g., over bed side rails) is more likely to result in injury because of the increased force of impact than a fall from a relatively low height, such as from a chair or toilet. Falls on hard, nonabsorptive floor surfaces such as linoleum tile, concrete, and wood are more likely to result in injury than falls onto absorptive surfaces such as carpeting.

Protective Reflexes

The onset of a fall elicits several protective reflexes: extending the arms outward and initiating quick shifting movements of the feet in order to regain balance. Both may avert a fall or minimize the force of impact. Conversely, a loss of protective reflexes stemming from neuromuscular dysfunction that affects the extremities or from sedation induced by medication may increase the impact of falling and the risk of injury.

"Shock Absorbers"

The presence of increased fat and muscle bulk surrounding vulnerable areas, such as the hip, is capable of absorbing the impact of a fall, decreasing the risk of fracture. Fractures are more likely to occur in people whose muscles have atrophied or who have a decreased amount of fat padding (e.g., thin people).

Bone Strength

A loss of bone strength attributable to osteoporosis at the femoral neck may result in fractures. These fractures may be either "spontaneous" hip fractures that occur during weight-bearing episodes or fractures that occur even with minimal ground impact against the bone. Bone loss is a particular problem in older women: By age 80, women may lose up to 50% of their bone strength, compared with 15% in men.

Immobility

In the absence of physical injury falls are often associated with a restriction of activities—either self- or staff-imposed—and immobility. As a consequence, people are at risk for a host of morbid complications that increase with the duration of immobility (Table 1-1). In turn, any

Table 1-1. Physiological and psychological consequences of immobility

System	Consequences
Musculoskeletal	Joint contractions, causing decreased range of motion Muscle weakness/atrophy Osteoporosis
Integumentary	Pressure sores
Respiratory	Pneumonia, causing decreased ventilation Pulmonary embolism
Cardiovascular	Orthostatic hypotension Venous stasis
Urinary	Urinary infections Incontinence
Gastrointestinal	Constipation
Neurological	Vestibular dysfunction / loss of balance
Psychological	Social isolation Decreased self-image Depression Anxiety Confusion

concomitant loss of functional status places individuals at additional risk for falls (Figure 1-1).

Psychosocial Trauma

Falls, particularly those that recur, are associated with a number of traumatic psychosocial consequences. Threats of impending falls can

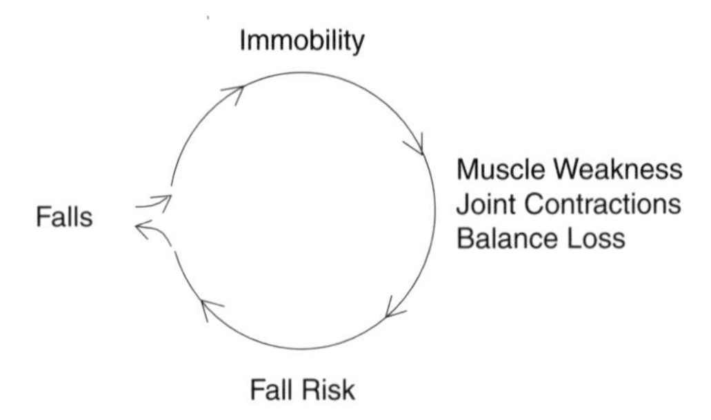

Figure 1-1. Falls that are associated with immobility and subsequent functional decline can increase the risk of additional falls.

alter self-image and create feelings of increasing frailty and incompetence. Often, people experience increased anxiety during the performance of the activities of daily living (ADLs; e.g., getting out of bed, transferring from the toilet) because they are uncertain as to whether the ADLs can be accomplished safely. Such people become increasingly apprehensive, and their sense of vulnerability to falling and self-injury is heightened. These individuals may become depressed, especially if their mobility or freedom to move about independently is diminished and they become functionally dependent on staff for assistance. Any limitations in mobility have broad lifestyle implications for these older adults. For example, they may remain in their room or sit alone on the unit, which decreases their sociability and participation in leisure activities. Often, compromised mobility that becomes permanent necessitates individuals being placed in a long-term care facility. Falls and immobility account for up to one third of all admissions to nursing facilities,[12] thus constituting one of the leading causes of nursing facility placement.

Patients and residents with falls may voice a number of other worries or fears, which include the following:

- Being belted or restrained, experiencing a loss of autonomy
- Having their relatives informed of the episode, which may cause further embarrassment for the patient or resident
- Being transferred to a "dependent" unit for their care, thus experiencing a loss of independence
- Fearing that nursing staff will not be available or come to their aid in time to prevent another fall from taking place
- Being forced to use a cane or walker, thus losing self-esteem
- Becoming a burden to family and staff members
- Dreading another injury, that the next fall will result in a hip fracture

Fear of Falling

Falls can lead to patients or residents losing confidence in their ability to function because of a fear of falling. Conservative estimates indicate that up to 50% of people who fall avoid ADLs because they fear additional falls and injury.[15] Such fear may be protective or it may be harmful. A certain degree may be protective if it motivates people to avoid activities to which they are no longer equal, to recognize their limitations, and to become more cautious. However, a fear of falling also can be detrimental, adversely affecting mobility and independence. As a response to their fear, some individuals alter their walking patterns; typically, their steps become hesitant and irregular. Ambulation is accompanied by a great deal of anxiety and often is accomplished by the person clutching or grabbing onto furnishings for support, a strategy that may increase the risk of falls. Subsequently, many people experience multiple near-falls, which can heighten their fear of falling and may lead to a curtailment of all physical activity. Devices that assist in safe mobility are often rejected because many older people are reluctant to project an image of frailty and thus endure social rejection from their peers, or they may feel that their cane or walker provides insufficient support. Other people who are fearful of falling may become chairbound or bedridden, reluctant to attempt independent activities and in need of human assistance to accomplish ADLs. Many patients and residents in this category develop a fear of being dropped by staff members during transfer activities and may be hesitant to leave their bed or chair.

Fear of falling may lead to a number of morbid outcomes. Older hospital patients may delay or eventually avoid discharge to the community, particularly if they live alone. Stalling can affect these patients adversely because many times it ultimately leads to placement in a nursing facility. Similarly, many nursing facility residents with a fear of falling become socially isolated and functionally dependent. Thus, the risk of complications associated with immobility increases.

FAMILY CONCERNS

Family members of people with falls in hospitals and nursing facilities also experience the consequences of falls. They may feel guilty about the fall, blaming themselves for not "being there" to prevent the event, or they may blame the nursing staff for allowing the fall to happen, sometimes even accusing the staff of neglect. Concerned for the safety of their relative, family members may insist on restricting activities and may inquire about the use of mechanical restraints and bed side rails to safeguard the patient or resident. These restrictions are especially likely to occur if the older person experiences multiple falls or a fall that results in injury. Although many family members become dismayed at the sight of restraints, they reluctantly accept their use for safety reasons. Other families, however, may insist on restraint removal, even if it places their loved ones at risk for falls. Families do not seek a guarantee that no harm will come to their relative, but rather assurance that the staff will assess the problem or the risk for subsequent falls and take appropriate measures to guard against falls. When alternatives to the use of mechanical restraints are discussed with family members, they often feel comfortable with the concept of reducing or eliminating restraints.

In the hospital setting, many families question staff about whether their loved ones can safely return home, particularly if they live alone. Families seek alternatives such as altered living arrangements (e.g., moving the relative with falls in with them) or placement in a group home or assisted living facility. If these options are not feasible, families may resort to nursing facility placement.

INSTITUTIONAL EFFECTS

The consequences of falls are also challenging for institutions. These complications include increased health care costs and effects on staff.

Health Care Costs

Falls and their complications often result in increased costs that arise from potential liability risks as well as health care needs. The institution and its employees are responsible for the safety of their patients or residents for the length of their stay in the institution, and thus may be held responsible if older adults fall and sustain injuries. Thus, both institution and staff are at risk for legal liability and increased costs associated with legal fees and settlement awards. Falls are the largest category of incident reports submitted to risk management for review because of potential liability.[13] The risk of legal action is highest in patients and residents whose falls are associated with serious injury, such as a fracture. Family members, rather than the patients and residents themselves, are likely to file a complaint against the institution, perhaps partly because of guilt about their relative's poor outcome.

Falls and injuries generate other expenses as well. These costs consist of

- Labor costs—Nursing, physician, and rehabilitative services accrued as a result of the time spent evaluating fall events, completing documentation (e.g., filling out occurrence reports, charting), providing postfall care (e.g., treating injury and immobility complications, restorative care), and monitoring patients and residents at fall risk (e.g., hourly nursing rounds, in-room sitters)

- Equipment costs—Mobility devices (e.g., canes, walkers, wheelchairs), bed rails, and durable medical equipment (e.g., grab bars, toileting devices, restraints, restraint-alternative devices)
- Utilization costs—Prolonged hospitalization (e.g., increased length of stay, increased bed-days) and permanent placement, in the case of nursing facilities; recurrent falls and their complications are common causes of rehospitalization and readmission to nursing facilities

Many times institutions must bear the brunt of these expenses. Hospital reimbursement systems may not pay for services required or extended days due to complications that stem from falls and injuries. Nursing facilities with reimbursement capitation, the necessary care that results from fall-related complications, may exceed coverage. In general, hospitals and nursing facilities that hold capitation contracts with managed care organizations are responsible for any expenses accumulated, and managed care plans that enroll residents of nursing facilities are responsible for covering fall-related costs.

Effects on Staff

Nursing staff caring for patients and residents with recurrent falls may find the responsibility of constantly deciding between the individuals' desire for autonomy and the families' requests for safety and guarding against the risk of falls emotionally demanding. Staff easily can become disheartened when patients and residents continue to fall, despite all their attempts to prevent falls. Often, they may experience stress, guilt, and self-doubt about their ability to deliver safe care.

NOTES

[1]Davis, A.E. (1995). Hip fractures in the elderly: Surveillance methods and injury control. *Journal of Nursing Trauma*, 2(1), 15–21.

[2]Centers for Disease Control and Prevention. (1995). *Injury mortality*, 1986–1992. Atlanta: Author.

[3]Centers for Disease Control and Prevention. (1996). *National summary of injury mortality data*, 1988–1994. Atlanta: Author.

[4]Baker, S.P., O'Neill, B., Ginsburg, M.J., & Guohua, L. (1992). *The injury fact book*. New York: Oxford University Press.

[5]Rubenstein, L.Z., Josephson, K.P., & Osterweil, D. (1996). Falls and fall prevention in the nursing home. *Clinics in Geriatric Medicine*, 12(4), 881–902.

[6]Wolinsky, F.D., Johnson, R.J., & Fitzgerald, J.F. (1992). Falling, health status, and use of health services by older adults. *Medical Care*, 30, 587–597.

[7]Miles, S.H., & Irvine, P.I. (1992). Deaths caused by physical restraints. *Gerontologist*, 32, 762–766.

[8]Sattin, R.W. (1992). Falls among older persons: A public health perspective. *Annual Review of Public Health*, 13, 489–508.

[9]U.S. Department of Health and Human Services, Public Health Service, National Center for Health Statistics. (1992). Unpublished data from the 1988 and 1991 National Hospital Discharge Survey. Washington, DC: Author.

[10]Fisher, E.S., Baron, J., Malenka, D.I., Barrett, J.A., Kniffin, W.D., Whaley, F.S., & Bubolz, T.A. (1991). Hip fracture mortality in New England. *Epidemiology*, 2(2), 116–122.

[11]Kennedy, E.M. (1994). *Hip fracture outcomes in people age fifty and over—Background paper*. OTA-BP-H-120. Washington, DC: U.S. Government Printing Office.

[12]Tinetti, M.E., & Speechley, M. (1989). Prevention of falls among the elderly. *New England Journal of Medicine*, 320, 1055–1059.

[13]Quinlan, W.C. (1994). The liability risk of patients who fall. *Journal of Healthcare Risk Management*, 14, 29–33.

[14]Melton, L.J., Chao, E.Y.S., & Lane, J. (1988). Biomechanical aspects of fractures. In B.L. Briggs & L.J. Melton (Eds.), *Osteoporosis: Etiology, diagnosis, and management* (pp. 111–131). New York: Raven Press.

[15]Franzoni, S., Ronzzini, R., Boffelli, S., Frisoni, E.B., & Trabucchi, M. (1994). Fear of falling in nursing home patients. *Gerontology*, 40, 38–44.

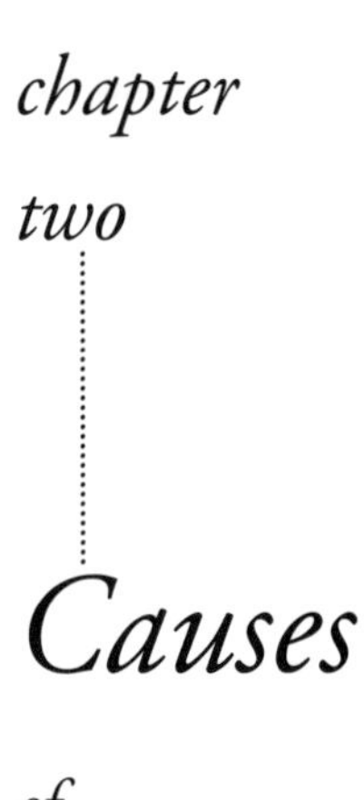

Causes of Falling and Fall Risk

A fall can be defined as any event in which a person inadvertently or intentionally comes to rest on the ground or another low level such as a chair, toilet, or bed. As an initial step in designing any planned intervention to reduce falls, it is essential to know why falls occur and under what circumstances they take place. The risk of falling occurs when an individual engages in an activity that results in a loss of balance, a displacement of the body beyond its base of support. Loss of balance may occur while carrying out everyday activities such as walking; transferring on or off chairs, wheelchairs, beds, and toilets; and reaching up or bending to retrieve or place objects. A fall is likely to follow an episode of balance loss if the neuromuscular systems responsible for balance stability fail to recognize and correct the displacement of the body in time to avert a fall.

Terminology

Agnosia	Neurological disorder that leads to disturbances in the recognition or perception of familiar sensory information
Cardiac arrhythmia	Any deviation from the normal pace of the heart
Apraxia	Loss of the ability to execute previously learned motor skills
Ataxia	Impairment of coordination of muscular activity
Cardioacceleration	An increase in the pulse rate
Cervical spondylosis	Breakdown of cervical vertebrae
Chronic obstructive pulmonary disease	General term for disease involving airway obstruction (e.g., chronic bronchitis, emphysema, asthma)

Falls in older people are often precipitated by a number of factors. These factors encompass intrinsic (e.g., age-related physiologic changes, disease states, medications) as well as extrinsic factors (e.g., hazardous environmental conditions, faulty devices, footwear). In addition, several situational circumstances, such as length of stay in institutional settings, time of day when falls take place, and staff characteristics influence the occurrence of falls.

The falling event should be viewed as a nonspecific sign or symptom representative of an underlying problem that can be attributed to either intrinsic or extrinsic factors. In the past, falls have been assigned to a single cause and ascribed either to a medical event or "accidental" environmental encounter. As researchers are beginning to understand, in general, falls in older people are not the result of a single intrinsic or extrinsic factor occurring in isolation; rather falls are complex events caused by a combination of both factors (Figure 2-1). However, for ease of understanding the etiology, or causes, of falls, it is useful to divide falls into strict intrinsic and extrinsic categories.

Congestive heart failure	Chronic inability of the heart to maintain an adequate output of blood, resulting in an inadequate blood supply to the body
Contrast sensitivity	The ability to perceive spatial detail and object contrast
Dark adaptation	The ability of the eyes to adjust to low levels of illumination
Dorsiflexion	Bending or flexing
Dysarthria	Difficulty in articulating single sounds in speech
Dysphasia	Disturbance in speech evidenced by lack of coordination and failure to express words in proper order
Electrolyte disorders	Disorder in compounds that play an essential role in function of the body
Extracellular volume regulation	Homeostatic mechanisms that regulate against volume depletion

Instrinsic Factors

A number of intrinsic factors play an important role in fall causation. These factors consist of age-related changes (e.g., changes in vision, changes in balance, changes in gait, changes in the musculoskeletal system, changes in the cardiovascular system), pathological conditions (e.g., acute diseases, chronic diseases), and medications.

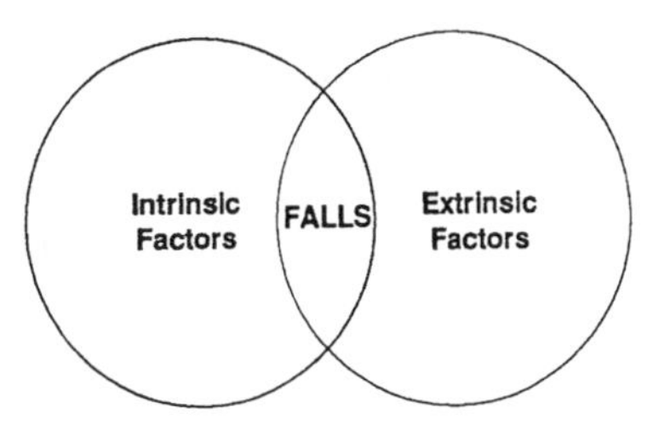

Figure 2-1. Falls are caused by the interaction of intrinsic and extrinsic factors.

Age-Related Changes

Mobility, the ability to maintain upright posture and to ambulate and transfer effectively, depends on the operation and integrity of many systems, primarily the visual, neurological, musculoskeletal, and cardiovascular systems. With advancing

Extrinsic	External to the system
Gait cycle	The manner of progression in walking or style of walking
Glare	A dazzling effect associated with a source of intense illumination
Hemianopsia	Blindness in half of the visual field
Hemiplegia	Paralysis involving one side of the body, generally an arm or leg
Hypotension	Low blood pressure
Hypovolemia	Low fluid states in the body
Intrinsic	Integral to the system
Kyphosis	Dorsal curvature of the spine in the thoracic area (i.e., hunchback)
Low contrast objects	Objects whose color is similar or indistinguishable from the immediate background
Macular degeneration	Eye condition, probably hereditary, causing diminished central vision

age, these systems decline gradually in function; they affect gait and balance and influence the risk of falling.

Changes in Vision

The ability of the eyes to adjust to varying levels of light and darkness diminishes as people age. The result is that the eyes of older people require more time to adjust to changes in environmental lighting. Dark adaptation is especially affected by aging and may compromise a person's visual capacity, particularly under conditions of low illumination (e.g., walking about or toileting during nighttime hours). When moving from a dimly lit room into bright lighting and vice versa, people often experience temporary blindness until the eyes adjust to the dramatic change in illumination.

A greater sensitivity of the aging eye to glare can lead to visual dysfunction. Common sources of glare include sunlight shining through windows and reflecting off waxed floors or glossy tabletops and bright

Marker	Early sign or indication of a corollary or subsequent event/disease
Nocturia	Excessive nighttime urination
Orthostatic hypotension	Lowered blood pressure that occurs on rising to an erect position
Osteomalacia	Softening of the bones
Paresis	Slight or incomplete paralysis; weakness
Peripheral neuropathy	Disease of the nerves
Polypharmacy	Use of multiple medications
Prodromal falls	Falling events that precede an episode of illness
Proprioception	Provides the body with kinesthetic information on the immediate environment, which enables the body to orient itself in space without visual clues; proprioception emerges from muscles, tendons, and joint receptors
Propulsion	An uncontrolled forward motion

light from unshielded light and fluorescent bulbs directed toward the eye. Glare from floor surfaces is particularly troublesome in that it can mask potential ground surface hazards. Also, glare can create visual distortions in older people that may result in their perceiving floor surfaces as excessively slippery. As a consequence, individuals sometimes alter their gait to compensate. They walk slower and more flat-footed and use a wider base of support, a pattern reminiscent of that which people adopt to walk on ice. However, this gait change may not be safe and may be hazardous in that it may lead to unsteadiness and falls. At other times, people cope with the glare emanating from floors by avoiding the surface altogether.

Restriction of a person's visual field leads to an inability to see objects in the pathway that lies outside the person's view, increasing the likelihood of slips and trips. A loss of visual acuity and contrast sensitivity can make the perception of objects in the environment more difficult. In particular, the detection of low-contrast objects can lead to unsafe ambulation and transferring activity. If not visualized clearly,

Proximal muscles	Muscles of the thighs, upper arms, and shoulders
Retropulsion	Loss of balance in a backward direction
Step length	The distance the foot travels during the swing phase
Steppage height	The level of ground clearance by the foot during the swing phase
Syncope	Fainting; temporary unconsciousness
Synergistic effects of medications	Accumulated effects of multiple medications
Vasomotor instability	Caliber of blood vessels affected
Vestibular input	Signals linear (angular) acceleration of the head; contributes to balance maintenance
Vestibular receptors	The semicircular canals and otolith organs located in the ear

objects such as extended chair and table legs, door thresholds, and carpet edges can cause people to trip. Furnishing surfaces (e.g., chair and toilet seats, bed mattress edges) that are not visually distinguishable can interfere with the achievement of proper stable seating positions, which increase the likelihood of falls while transferring. The loss of visual acuity and contrast sensitivity is more evident under conditions of low illumination.

A decline in depth perception can cause the visual detection of ground surfaces (e.g., patterned or checkered linoleum, carpet designs) to appear to be elevations or depressions on the ground, surfaces that older people prefer to step around or avoid walking on entirely. In addition, a loss of depth perception makes it difficult to perceive objects that lie in areas of shadows, low illumination, or excessive brightness.

Changes in Balance

The body's ability to maintain balance depends on the central nervous and musculoskeletal systems, requiring adequate vision, proprioceptive feedback, vestibular input, muscle strength, and joint flexibility to detect and correct balance displacement. Combined, these systems culminate in postural sway, a process of anteroposterior and lateral motion of the erect or seated body that controls stability and protects against the forces of gravity.

Balance is achieved by the body's continual positioning of its center of gravity over a base of support: the feet, when standing (Figure 2-2), and the buttocks, when sitting (Figure 2-3). When performing an activity such as walking or transferring, the center of gravity extends beyond the base of support and stretches beyond the limits of stability (Figure 2-4). The resulting imbalance is detected by the visual, vestibular, and proprioceptive components of the central nervous system, which sends signals to stretch receptors located in the joints and muscles of the legs. This signaling initiates a set of coordinated protective movements (e.g., a forward or backward shifting of the feet while standing or walking, a widening of the feet while seated or transferring) that pulls the body's center of gravity into alignment with its base of support.

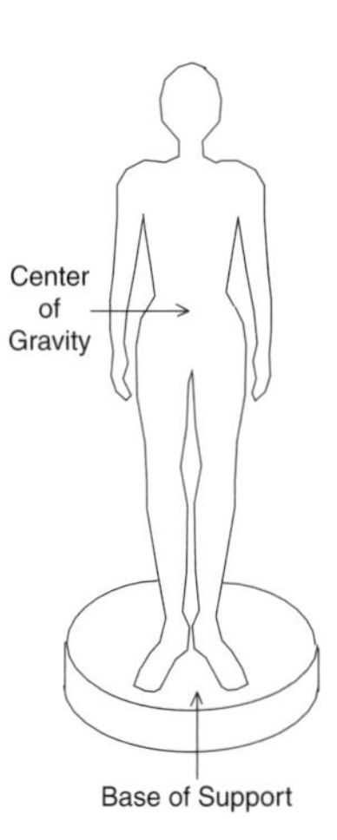

Figure 2-2. The center of gravity in relationship to the base of support when standing.

As people age, the capabilities of the proprioceptive system decline, and, as a consequence, postural sway increases. Vision can augment proprioceptive feedback or counteract its loss. To compensate for poor balance, many individuals ambulate by looking down to view the correct placement of their feet; to ensure proper transferring, they constantly view the surface on which they sit. Vision is a mainstay of balance. The eyes provide the body with information on the placement of and distance from objects in the environment, the type of surface on which movement will take place, the position of the body, and the intensity of effort or degree of difficulty of the required movement. Vision also provides the information the person needs to think ahead of time and gauge the timing and control of movement. The more difficult the activity or the greater the precision and speed needed to accomplish

Figure 2-3. The center of gravity in relationship to the base of support when seated.

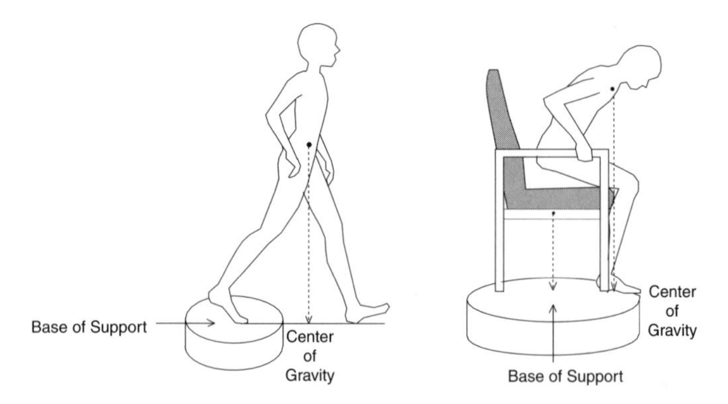

Figure 2-4. The center of gravity in relationship to the base of support during (left) ambulation and (right) transfers.

the movement, the greater the importance of vision. When visual input is diminished by age-related changes, balance becomes difficult to maintain. This concept is demonstrated when an older person stands with his or her eyes closed or walks into a dark room; in both cases, balance is unsteady.

The vestibular system works in conjunction with the visual and proprioceptive systems to achieve balance—it helps to maintain stable visual perception and body orientation as a person moves about the environment. During periods of displacement of balance, the vestibular receptors detect movement and prompt antigravity extensor muscles to execute compensatory head, trunk, and limb movements, which serve to oppose postural sway. In other words, the system located in the inner ear that regulates balance senses that the body has been placed out of balance and signals the neuromuscular system to activate one or more movements to ensure that a fall does not take place. This body-orienting response, known as the righting reflex, diminishes with age. Consequently, when an older person slips or trips or loses balance while transferring, his or her chance of regaining stability and avoiding a fall declines.

Normally, some redundancy occurs in the sensory information necessary to maintain balance, and the failure of one source of input such as vision can be counteracted with feedback from intact proprioceptive and vestibular systems. However, deprivation in more than one system is likely to lower the balance threshold and increase fall risk. This risk becomes evident when older people who fall are compared with older

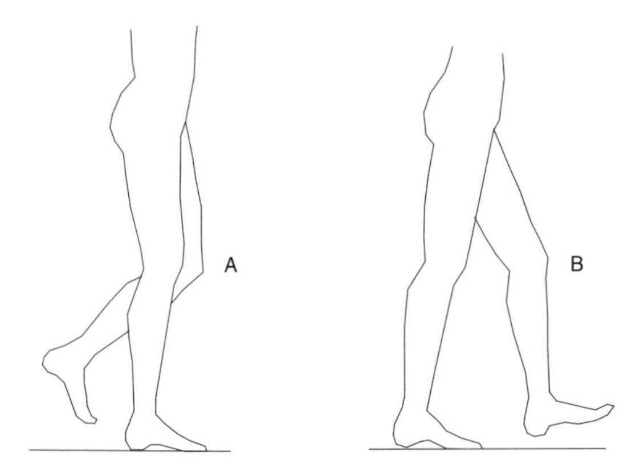

Figure 2-5. (A) The stance phase and (B) the swing phase of the gait cycle.

people without falls. Older people who fall have greater postural sway or unsteadiness than individuals without falls, and people with multiple falls demonstrate appreciably more sway than those with single falls.[1]

Changes in Gait

The gait cycle consists of two phases: stance and swing. The stance phase occurs when one leg is in contact with the ground and the swing phase occurs when the other leg is advanced forward to take the next step (Figure 2-5). Ambulation is accomplished via a series of reciprocal leg movements that alternate between stance and swing—pushing off on the leg in stance phase while swinging the other leg forward. To allow for adequate ground clearance during the swing phase, the leg is flexed at the knee and dorsiflexed at the foot (Figure 2-6). When the heel of the swing leg strikes the ground, the return to the stance phase, the knee is extended and the foot plantar is flexed to provide support to the body (Figure 2-7).

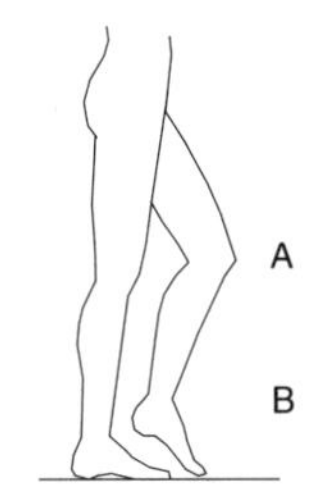

Figure 2-6. Ground clearance during the swing phase is accomplished by (A) knee flexion and (B) ankle dorsiflexion.

As compared with younger people, older individuals experience a number of changes in the gait cycle. The speed of walking, step length, and steppage height declines (Figure 2-8). Changes in gait are also specific to each gender, although

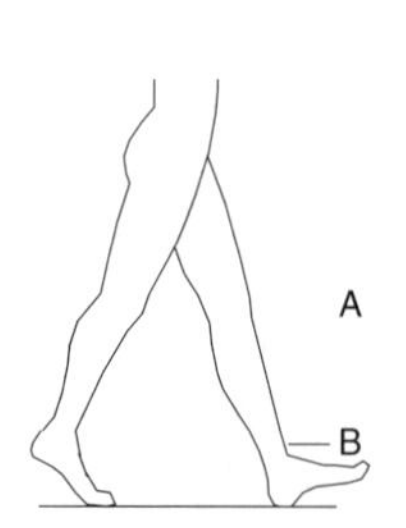

Figure 2-7. Ground support during a return to the stance phase is accomplished by (A) knee extension and (B) ankle plantar flexion.

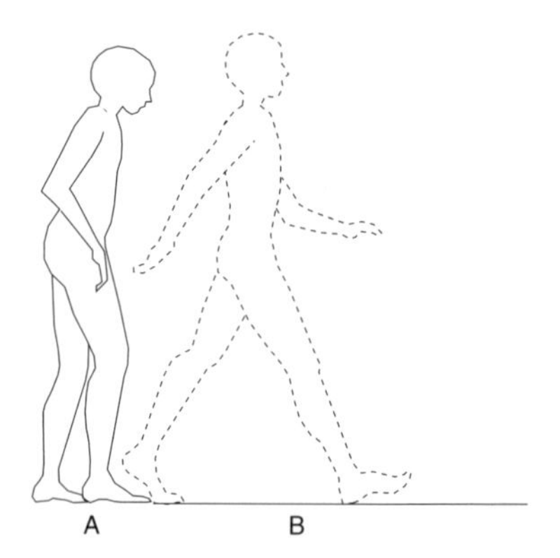

Figure 2-8. The gait of (A) an older person is compared with that of (B) a younger person, demonstrating a decrease in step length and steppage height.

they are not well understood. Women tend to develop a narrow standing and walking base, often take small steps, and exhibit a pelvic waddle during ambulation. The pelvic waddle has been attributed, in part, to a loss of muscular control in the lower extremities. Conversely, older men tend to adopt a wide standing and walking base and assume a more shuffling type of gait.

Whether age-related changes in gait are compensatory and serve to maintain balance or are hazardous, and thus influence fall risk, remains speculative. Alterations in gait, however, are more evident in people with a history of falls and this influences fall susceptibility to a certain degree. When the swing phase is interrupted (Figure 2-9), either the foot fails to adequately clear the ground or it encounters an irregularity on the surface of the floor such as curled-up carpeting or a raised tile edge, resulting in a trip. When a bare foot or shoe bottom either encounters a surface of low frictional resistance (e.g., wet or highly polished floor surface) or approaches the ground with a change in stride length during a return to the stance phase, a slip can occur (Figure 2-10). Whether a trip or slip results in a fall depends on the ability of the individual to initiate and execute maneuvers that correct his or her balance.

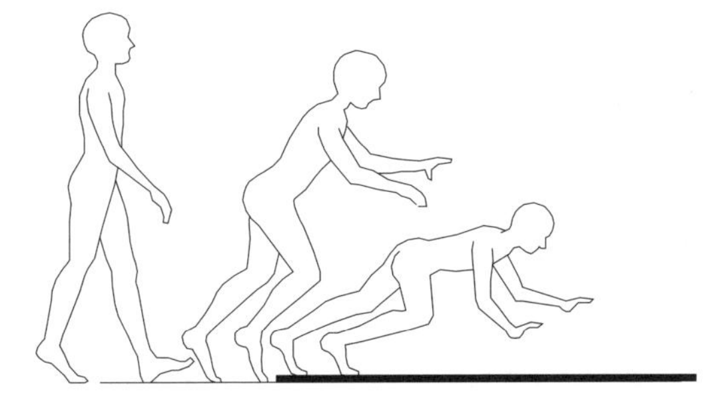

Figure 2-9. The movement of the right foot is interrupted during the swing phase. A trip and fall forward occurs as a result.

Changes in the Musculoskeletal System

The capacity to maintain balance while walking and transferring, and thus accomplish these activities safely, is affected by a number of age-related changes in the musculoskeletal system. Such changes include muscle atrophy, calcification of tendons and ligaments, and increased curvature of the spine due to osteoporosis, which results in kyphosis. In response, older people develop a stooped posture (Figure 2-11), and thus experience difficulty extending their hips and knees fully when

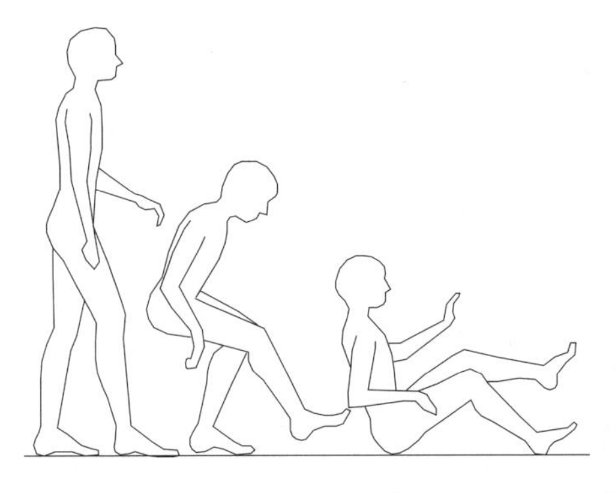

Figure 2-10. The movement of the right foot during a return to the stance phase encounters a surface of low frictional resistance. A slip and fall backward occurs as a result.

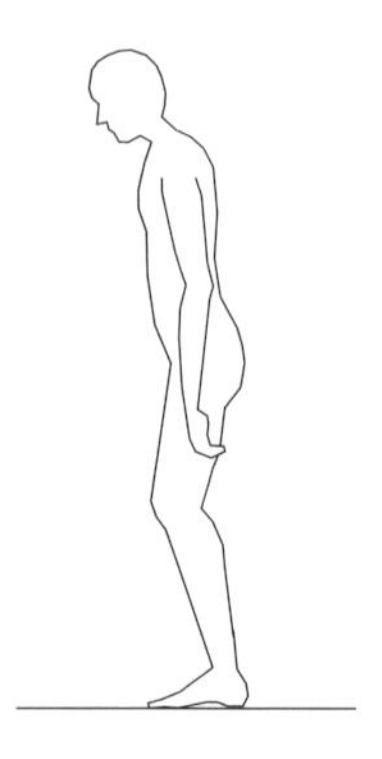

Figure 2-11. Age-related musculoskeletal changes can lead to a stooped posture.

walking. This response to postural changes can affect their ability to maintain stability and to correct any displacements of balance that may occur. A severe forward-leaning posture may alter the body's balance threshold: The center of gravity is shifted forward, past the base of support (i.e., the critical point of stability), making it more difficult for older people to thrust the foot forward quickly enough to preserve balance. Poor ankle muscle strength complicates the execution, and older people find it difficult to adjust their center of gravity in line with the base of support rapidly enough to prevent a fall. In fact, with age, general muscular strength declines, particularly in the proximal muscles.

The deterioration of articular cartilage in the hips and knees becomes prominent in older adults. In concert, these changes can impair transfer activity (e.g., sitting down and rising from chairs, toilets, and beds). An inability to flex the knees and hips sufficiently and the loss of lower-extremity strength may impair the capacity of the legs to exert maximum push or force during the attempt to transfer. Similarly, a decrease in shoulder flexibility and strength may cause the body to fail to provide optimal upper extremity leverage during transfers.

Changes in the Cardiovascular System

Aging is associated with several physiological changes that impair homeostasis or regulation of blood pressure, which can predispose older adults to falls. The baroreceptor reflex, which consists of stretch receptors located in large arteries, is sensitive to sudden changes in blood pressure and serves as a regulatory mechanism that helps to maintain sufficient blood flow to the brain. This reflex occurs despite changes in posture, such as suddenly standing up after remaining seated or in a prone position for some time. As people age they experience a progressive decline in baroreflex stimulation, which is due to arteriosclerosis. This arterial hardening may cause transient episodes of hypotension, which becomes evident in the presence of hypotensive stimuli such as hypovolemia (e.g., dehydration, blood loss) or medication side effects. As such, the aged heart is less able than a younger heart to cardioaccelerate to compensate for any hypotensive effects. Also, older people have impaired extracellular volume regulation and, as a result, sodium conservation declines. Diminished sodium conservation can lead to sodium imbalance and dehydration, which can influence blood pressure regulation and subsequently lead to hypotension.

Pathological Conditions

Diseases and their associated impairments, superimposed on age-related physiological changes, play a more decisive role in falls than do physiological changes occurring by themselves. Older people possess considerable reserve capacity beyond what may be needed for ordinary mobility tasks. Therefore, aging per se and age-related physiological changes are less likely to cause falls in the absence of associated disease. Often, falls are markers for an underlying acute disease or diseases. Indeed, evidence indicates that, in general, people with repeated falls have more medical comorbidity than do individuals without falls.[2]

Acute Diseases

A falling event may be the initial sign or an early indication of an underlying acute illness, representing the onset of new diseases or unstable existing disease, as in the following case example:

B.R. *is an* 89-*year-old man with severe* Parkinson's *disease who experienced five falls during a* 2-*week period. The falls were ascribed to poor mobility, resulting from his neurological disease. Subsequent investigation, however, revealed the presence of a gastrointestinal bleed (i.e., blood in the stool with anemia), which was generated by a stomach ulcer. Upon treatment of the ulcer, his falls ceased.*

Falling episodes that precede an episode of illness are referred to as *prodromal falls*. Illnesses most often identified as causative of falls are those present at the time of the fall that interfere with postural stability; such illnesses include syncope, hypotension, cardiac arrhythmias, electrolyte disorders, seizures, stroke, febrile conditions (e.g., urinary tract infections, pneumonia), and acute exacerbations of underlying chronic diseases (e.g., congestive heart failure, chronic obstructive pulmonary disease, kidney failure).

Chronic Diseases

Frequently, a fall heralds a deterioration in health that is attributable to a chronic disease. Disease processes that predispose to falls include any persistent physical condition that interferes with mobility (e.g., the ability to walk about the environment; safe transfer on and off chairs, beds, and toilets). The most common disease processes originate in the visual, neurological, and musculoskeletal systems. Degenerative cognitive disorders compound the effects of falls and create a high risk for them.

Visual Disorders Diseases of the eye such as cataracts, macular degeneration, glaucoma, and hemianopsia interfere with visual fields and decrease visual perception, visual acuity, and dark adaptation. Cataracts result in an overall blurring of vision, causing images to appear hazy or cloudy, and cause increased sensitivity to glare. Macular degeneration affects only central vision; peripheral vision remains intact. Glaucoma results in the loss of peripheral vision, and hemianopsia causes loss of vision in half of the visual field. When combined with poor illumination, visual disorders can result in poor recognition of environmental ground hazards and predispose individuals to trips and slips.

Neurological Disorders Dementia, especially of the Alzheimer's type, is associated with neurological disorders: ataxia, proprioceptive loss, apraxia, visuospatial dysfunction in object recognition, and agnosia. These changes lead to misinterpretation of environmental conditions, resulting in trips and slips, balance loss, and a reduced ability to correct imbalance and falls.

Neuropathy, the result of conditions such as diabetes mellitus, vitamin B_{12} deficiency, and cervical spondylosis, is associated with lower-extremity weakness and altered proprioception, which can lead to poor balance and abnormal gait. Lower-extremity hemiplegia or paresis resulting from stroke can result in a narrow, unstable standing and walking base of support, which is maintained typically on the unaffected foot, and increases the risk of loss of balance. A decrease in ankle dorsiflexion of the affected limb results in a diminished ability to initiate quick postural responses, and reduced foot–ground clearance during ambulation precipitates tripping. Parkinsonism affects postural control; it institutes a loss of autonomic postural reflexes, propulsion, retropulsion, and certain gait changes (e.g., short-stepping and shuffling, barely clearing the ground; poor initiation; freezing or sudden halting of gait) that can lead to a displaced center of gravity, loss of balance, and fall risk.

Musculoskeletal Disorders Proximal muscle weakness, concomitant with conditions such as thyroid disease, polymyalgia rheumatica, osteomalacia, or deconditioning, can lead to unstable, waddling gaits and problems with transferring. Osteoarthritis of the knees and hips with limited joint flexibility may result in similar problems. Disorders of the foot (e.g., toe deformities, calluses, bunions) lead to mechanical problems during ambulation and unsteady gaits.

Cognitive Disorders Altered thought processes resulting from dementia or depression are associated with falls. Older adults may misperceive environmental dangers, err in judgment, or fail to discriminate between safe and dangerous environmental conditions or activities. Consequently, they may place themselves in hazardous situations and take chances that people who are cognitively intact would avoid. Individuals with dementia who wander, especially those with mobility problems, can be at particular risk, and they may lack the ability to communicate their needs. Conversely, despite their functional frailty, some people who are cognitively intact insist on maintaining a risky level of autonomy, particularly if they are accustomed to being active and independent. Their stubbornness can increase the risk of falls.

Language Disorders Impaired communication attributable to conditions such as dysarthria and dysphagia may seriously compromise an older adult's safety. An inability to make one's wishes known (e.g., needing help with bed transfers, walking to the bathroom) or an inability to understand safety risks causes individuals to attempt activities when they may be inadvisable or risky. In addition, any frustration or anxiety resulting from a failure to communicate can increase the risk of falls. Avoiding a fall is likely not the primary concern of people who are frustrated or anxious. Rather, they become consumed emotionally by an immediate problem, such as toileting. As a result, individuals may be less alert to surrounding environmental hazards.

The management of patients and residents with communication deficits consists of identifying the language problems and any specific precautions needed to ensure their safety. In general, older adults need to be informed about hazardous activities and environmental conditions, as well as about ways to call for help when it is needed, despite the difficulty in communicating. The use of pictures, pantomime, notebooks, communication boards, and cards that have pictures of familiar objects should be encouraged. A speech-language pathologist can help to identify other communication-enhancing techniques.

Medications[3-5]

Physiologic responses to medications change as people age. A number of pharmacokinetic and pharmacodynamic changes take place, affecting how the body handles a drug, as well as the specific action of the drug on the body. Major pharmacokinetic alterations in the distribution, metabolism, and excretion of medications occur with aging. An increase in total body fat and decrease in lean muscle mass cause alterations in lipophilic, or fat-soluble, medications. For example, benzodiazepines and psychotropic medications delay clearance from the body and prolong the half-life of drugs. A decrease in total body water and albumin levels may lead to high serum levels of medications, or accumulation of water-soluble and protein-binding drugs. The capacity of the liver to metabolize medications is also impaired, the effect being acute with benzodiazepines. A reduction in hepatic blood flow can decrease the clearance of drugs traveling through the liver, thus prolonging their half-lives. Psychotropics appear to be affected the most by the aging metabolism. A reduction in renal blood flow and glomerular filtration rate in the kidney leads to a decreased excretion of drugs that are eliminated renally.

Pharmacodynamic changes, which influence the onset, duration, and intensity of drug action or the response to a given dosage, are attributed to alterations occurring at organ system receptor sites. The central nervous system and cardiovascular system receptor sites are affected the most profoundly with regard to postural stability. Drug action is enhanced for most medications within the central nervous system, particularly for psychoactive drugs because of degenerative changes in brain matter and the neurotransmitters. An increase in body sway or unsteadiness has been demonstrated to occur shortly after the administration of psychotropic medications. In the cardiovascular system, a decline in baroreflex activity increases the body's sensitivity to antihypertensive agents and contributes to the risk of postural hypotension.

Taken together, pharmacokinetic and pharmacodynamic alterations make older people susceptible to drug interactions and side effects that enhance the risk of falls and injury. The classes of medications associated most commonly with falls include diuretics, hypnotics and sedatives, antidepressants, psychotropics, and antihypertensives. Any of these drugs can interfere with postural control, motor and sensory coordination, or cognitive function, which may adversely influence gait and balance and induce a fall. Other medications, such as nonsteroidal anti-inflammatory agents (NSAIDs) and laxatives, have been implicated as a cause of falls. Their action is not direct but is contributory, adding to the effects of underlying arthritis or a mobility dysfunction. Thus, older people may exceed their capabilities, for example, when rushing to the bathroom, and fall.

The risk of falling is greatest when taking drugs with extended half-lives (greater than 24 hours) and increases with the number of medications a person consumes. In principle, the risk of falls and injury should always be taken into consideration when medications are prescribed. Particular care must be taken with drugs that have the potential for adverse effects on cognitive function and/or gait and balance. Although these medications may be acceptable for treating the underlying problem, their side effects can increase the risk of falls and injury (Figure 2-12).

Extrinsic Factors

A number of extrinsic factors play an important role in fall causation. These factors consist of the physical environment, the design of furnishings, the condition of ground surfaces, and illumination. In addition, several devices used to promote mobility (e.g., walkers, wheelchairs) or guard against falls (e.g., mechanical restraints, bed side rails) have been implicated in causing falls. Also, the type and condition of footwear worn by patients and residents can play a primary role in fall causation.

Physical Environment

The majority of institutional falls experienced by older patients and residents occur in the bedroom, bathroom, and dining areas, reflecting the amount of time people spend in these areas.[6] In conjunction with patient- or resident-initiated activities, several environmental obstacles and design features are associated with falls: transferring from inap-

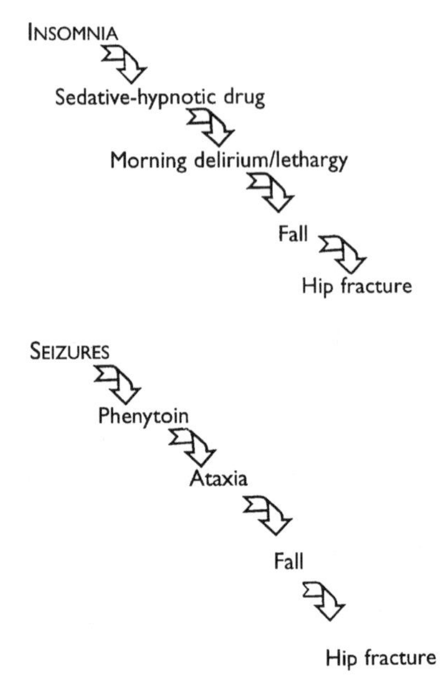

Figure 2-12. Example of medications prescribed for the treatment of medical problems such as insomnia and seizures and the potential side effects leading to falls and injury.

propriately low or high bed heights or climbing over bed side rails; sitting on and rising from low-seated, unstable, armless chairs and low-seated toilets lacking grab bar support; walking in poorly illuminated areas and tripping over low-lying objects or floor coverings, such as thick-pile carpeting and upended linoleum or tile flooring; and slipping on highly polished or wet ground surfaces and sliding rugs. The probability of the physical environment contributing to falls is highest for individuals with mobility problems (e.g., altered gait and balance, impaired transfers), wherein the physical demands of activities or tasks may exceed the competence of the individual.

Relocation—moving from home to hospital or nursing facility, from one facility to another, from hospital to nursing facility and vice versa, or from one hospital unit to another—can increase the risk of falls. New environments can affect frail older people adversely, particularly individuals with mobility problems. Also, people with dementia may not tolerate change well, increasing their confusion and their risk of falls. Relocation to a new environment, which includes unfamiliar surroundings, new roommates, social situations, and nursing and other staff, and changes in daily activities, can be stressful and potentially disorienting for people with dementia.

Devices

Devices such as bed side rails and mechanical restraints are often used with people who are at risk for falls in an attempt to protect them. It is ironic that these devices may actually increase fall risk in some instances. When patients or residents exit the bed by climbing over elevated bed side rails, perhaps catching their arms or legs in the rails, transferring activity becomes dangerous and increases fall risk (Figure 2-13). Also, individuals are more susceptible to injury, such as a fracture, when a fall from a great height occurs. In addition, bed side rails are associated with a host of other injuries, such as soft tissue bruises, contusions, lacerations, and fractures. These injuries result from becoming entrapped in bed side rails, bumping into rails, or falling between the mattress and bed side rail while a person attempts to get out of bed. Bed side rails have been known to break or become unhitched from bed frames during transfers. Most bed side rail injuries are associated with full-length rails. However, this statement does not imply that half side rails are benign.

The use of mechanical restraints can contribute to falls. When applied improperly, restraints can be untied or slipped out of by older adults. As a result they can fall from chairs and wheelchairs or out of

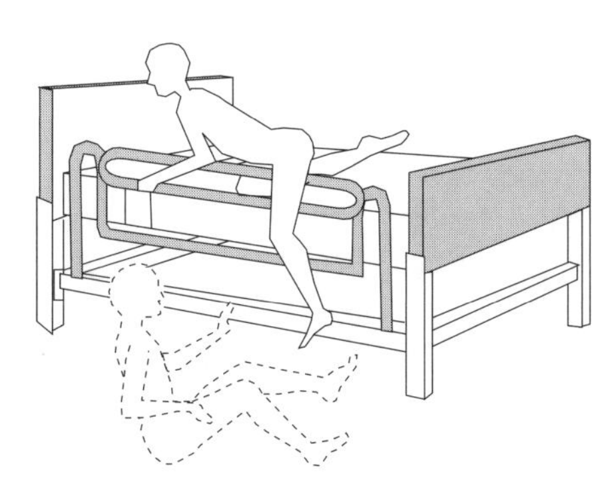

Figure 2-13. Transfers over elevated bed side rails can increase fall risk.

bed. Patients and residents also may become entangled in restraints while attempting to get out of bed. Using restraints may increase older adults' risk of falls because of the effects of immobilization caused by restraints devices (e.g., deconditioning, muscle weakness, loss of joint flexibility, vasomotor instability). In addition, restraints can lead to increased anxiety, anger, agitation, and confusion, which heighten risk for falls. Moreover, the effectiveness of mechanical restraints in preventing falls and related injuries is questionable. Restrained patients and residents experience more falls and serious fall-related injuries than do unrestrained individuals. Institutions that have limited their use of mechanical restraints have experienced either no increase in falls or only a slight increase. Any increase in falls that may result from eliminating restraints, however, is not accompanied by an increase in serious fall-related injuries.

Canes and walkers, devices prescribed to support mobility, can contribute to unsafe mobility if they are the wrong size, if they are used improperly, or if they are in a poor state of repair (e.g., worn rubber tips, structural breakdown). Patients and residents with inappropriate or malfunctioning walking devices may abandon or use their ambulation aid sparingly, which increases the risk of falls. Wheelchairs contribute to falls when a poor transfer technique (i.e., not locking wheel brakes, feet not clearing the footplates) is used. Wheelchairs may roll away or tip over during transfers. At other times, poor wheelchair design (e.g., inaccessibility of wheelchair brakes; short handles, improper footrest placement) and the condition of the chair itself (e.g., broken equipment, worn brakes and footrests) can be responsible for falls. In addition, falls from wheelchairs sometimes occur when patients and residents reach for objects or lean too far forward in their chairs, leading to wheelchair instability. People with cognitive and lower extremity problems are at special risk for wheelchair falls; for example, they do not remember to lock wheelchair brakes or they fail to clear the footplates when exiting the chair. Some individuals in wheelchairs who exhibit agitated behaviors may excessively rock their chairs to the point of tipping them over.

Footwear

Improper footwear can alter gait and balance and lead to falls. High-heeled shoes narrow the standing and walking base of support, decrease stride length, and place individuals in a forward-leaning posture, causing their balance to become precarious and making them susceptible to falls. Poorly fitting shoes, particularly loose shoes, can affect ambulation adversely. In an effort to keep their shoes on, people may shuffle when they walk, then trip. Leather-soled shoes promote slipping as does wearing socks without shoes. Rubber crepe soles, although slip-resistant, may stick to linoleum floor surfaces. Such sticking can halt gait precipitously, causing forward balance loss and falls, particularly in older adults with decreased foot–ground clearance. Thick-soled footwear such as running shoes or sneakers may decrease the proprioceptive feedback that is derived from striking the foot on the ground during ambulation and cause a loss of balance.

Situational Circumstances

Situational circumstances also are responsible for predisposing older adults to falls and for contributing to falls. The circumstances examined here are length of stay in the health care facility, time at which the fall occurs, and specific characteristics of the facility staff.

Length of Stay

Commonly, older adults fall during the first week and after the third week of institutional stay. Various explanations have been offered. Incidents during the first week may be attributable to lack of familiarity with the environment or the presence of acute (i.e., altered homeostasis) or chronic diseases (i.e., altered mobility). Hospital patients who fall after the third week may be—at least as perceived by both themselves and the staff—ready for discharge and allowed full mobility. Residents of nursing facilities with functional limitations requiring staff assistance at the time of admission can improve their functional status with restorative care and thus are allowed independent freedom of movement. However, they may not have recovered their mobility fully, placing them at certain fall risk, which may account for falls after the third week. In acute care hospitals, increased length of stay is positively correlated with an increase in falls, presumably due to a greater chance of iatrogenic (i.e., induced inadvertently by a physician or by medical treatment) factors contributing to the risk.

Time of Fall

Most falls occur during the night (i.e., 11 P.M.–7 A.M.) and select daylight hours (i.e., 6 A.M.–10 A.M.; 4 P.M.–8 P.M.). The primary explanation for nocturnal falls has been that older people get up to toilet, despite the fact that their ability to transfer safely out of bed is diminished and that they travel to the bathroom under poor illumination conditions. Also contributing to fall risk is that there is less staff available at night to assist patients and residents. The hours of peak frequency of falls during daylight hours corresponds to heightened waking activity levels.

Staff Characteristics

Staffing patterns, the number of nurses and nursing assistants available on any one shift, may also influence fall occurrence. Most research shows an inverse correlation between falls and the number of staff available; falls increase as staff is decreased and, as the number of staff increases, the frequency of falls declines. Sometimes the correlation is reversed; that is, falls increase with the addition of staff members. The reason for this reversed correlation is not entirely clear and may not relate strictly to the absolute number of nurses or to the ratio of staff to patients or residents, but rather to their availability and their attitudes toward assisting people who are mobility impaired. In other words, positive staff attitudes with respect to caring for older people may positively influence the occurrence of falls, and negative attitudes may lead to acts of omission (e.g., failure to assess for risk and implement preventive strategies), and thus, increased falls. Therefore, falls may not be related to the number of staff or ratio of staff to patients or residents but instead to the availability of staff at the time of the fall and the attitudes of the staff. Other complicating factors include the location of the rooms of people who fall, particularly if patients or residents reside a long distance from the nurses' station and time-consuming trips by staff are required, and the number of staff present on different nursing shifts, weekends, and during holidays.

Risk Factors for Falls and Injury

Although a number of intrinsic and extrinsic factors predispose older people to falls and injuries, the design of effective preventive measures is dependent on identifying the specific risk factors involved. Several host-related or intrinsic factors have been found repeatedly to be strongly associated with the risk of institutional falls:

Decreased vision (e.g., cataracts, macular degeneration, glaucoma, hemianopsia)

Lower-extremity dysfunction (e.g., arthritis, muscle weakness, peripheral neuropathy, foot disorders)
Gait/balance disorders (e.g., Parkinson's disease, stroke, cane/walker use)
Cardiovascular disorders (e.g., orthostatic hypotension, arrhythmia, syncope)
Bladder dysfunction (e.g., nocturia, incontinence, frequency of urination)
Cognitive dysfunction (e.g., dementia, depression, anxiety, fear of falling, denial of physical and functional limitations, refusal to use required assistive devices)
Communication disorders (e.g., dysarthria, dysphasia)
Medications (e.g., diuretics, antihypertensives, sedatives, psychotropics, NSAIDs, number of drugs or polypharmacy)

These factors, either in isolation or combination, contribute to altered mobility, the ability to achieve and maintain safe ambulation, transferring activities (e.g., on/off beds, chairs, toilets, wheelchairs), and bending/reaching activities (e.g., obtaining/placing objects; onto/from nightstands; into/from closets, cabinets, dressers), or the ability to ask for required assistance with mobility tasks.

Diseases associated with lower-extremity dysfunction contribute greatly to gait and balance problems. These diseases impair effective ambulation and the speed and reliability of postural reflexes to correct balance displacements. In addition, loss of lower-extremity strength is significantly associated with transfer difficulties that arise when sitting on or rising from chairs, beds, and toilets. Visual disorders can impair the detection of ground surfaces or low-lying environmental objects and can interfere with the physiological compensation that corrects balance instability. Cognitive disturbances influence how an individual perceives and adapts to the environment and activity demands. As a risk factor, urinary dysfunction is complex. Toileting requires people to rise from a bed or chair, ambulate to the bathroom, adjust their clothing, position themselves on the toilet, maintain their balance on the toilet, stand up, leave the bathroom, and return to the point of origin. A fall may occur at any time. In addition, there is a risk that on the way to the bathroom a person will become incontinent and slip in his or her urine. The synergistic effects of medications at inappropriate dosages and the overzealous use of hypnotic-anxiolytic agents contribute to gait and postural instability. The risk of falling increases with the number of intrinsic risk factors present; multiple risk factors are more likely to be present in individuals with recurrent falls than in people without recurrent falls. Furthermore, the risk of falls is greatly increased in patients and residents with a history of falls during the past 3 months and/or recurrent falls (i.e., multiple episodes occurring over a short period of time—days to weeks).

When these intrinsic risk factors are combined with undesirable environmental conditions or extrinsic factors, the risk of falling is increased further. For example, unsuitable environments such as low-seated furnishings and toilets, reduced illumination and hazardous ground surfaces may be negotiated easily by people who are functionally healthy. However, in individuals with altered mobility, the condition of the environment can be a major obstacle, leading to fall risk.

The risk of injury following a fall is heightened by the presence of the following factors:

Advanced age—Older women with osteoporosis are at particular risk

Lower-extremity weakness and loss of joint flexibility, and/or gait disturbances—Greater risk of balance loss and inability to recover balance

Ambulation with a cane or walker—Increased likelihood of gait or balance disorder

Poor vision—Inability to detect ground surface hazards, which can lead to trips and slips

Dementia—Errors in judgment between safe and hazardous tasks or the environment; reduced ability to correct imbalance

Immobility—Increased probability of lower-extremity weakness and joint inflexibility, resulting in balance loss and poor balance recovery

The risk of falls and injury occurs in three phases. Phase 1 is the initiating event that displaces the person's base of support and balance when walking. For patients and residents, these initiating events may be the result of lower-extremity dysfunction such as muscle weakness, unstable joints, diminished postural reflexes, or environmental hazards, such as a slippery floor surface. Phase 2 occurs when the person's systems for maintaining upright posture or balance stability fail to recognize and correct the balance displacement in time to avoid a fall. In older people a failure to recover balance during a fall may be due to a loss of sensory and motor functions, which may be the result of neurological and musculoskeletal disorders. Phase 3 of the fall, commonly referred to as the impact phase, occurs when the person hits the floor. It is during this phase that the forces of the impact are transmitted to the body, possibly resulting in an injury. Efforts to prevent falls and injury must begin at Phase 1; the cause of falls must be evaluated and fall risk must be assessed, and subsequently, an attempt must be made to modify the risk factors discovered in an effort to prevent the occurrence of Phases 2 and 3. This approach is examined in the chapters that follow.

NOTES

[1]Janken, J.K., & Reynolds, B.A. (1987). Identifying patients with the potential for falling. In A. McLane (Ed.), *Classification of nursing diagnosis* (pp. 136–143). St. Louis: Mosby.

[2]Myers, A.H., Baker, S.P., Van Natta, M.L., Abby, H., & Robinson, E.G. (1991). Risk factors associated with falls and injuries among elderly institutionalized persons. *American Journal of Epidemiology*, 133, 1179–1190.

[3]Campbell, A.J. (1991). Drug treatment as a cause of falls in old age: A review of the offending agents. *Drugs and Aging*, 1, 289–302.

[4]Ray, W.A., & Griffin, M.R. (1990). Prescribed medications and the risk of falling. *Topics in Geriatric Rehabilitation*, 5, 12–20.

[5]Thapa, P.B., & Ray, W.A. (1996). Medications and falls and fall-related injuries in the elderly. In A.M. Bronstein, T. Brandt, & M.H. Woollacott (Eds.), *Clinical disorders of balance, posture and gait* (pp. 301–325). London: Arnold.

[6]Connell, B.R. (1996). Role of the environment in falls prevention. *Clinics in Geriatric Medicine*, 12(4), 859–880.

chapter three

Clinical Assessment and Evaluation

The accumulated effects of multiple diseases, medications, and resulting disabilities, combined with extrinsic factors (i.e., environmental settings that are hazardous or unsuitable for safe mobility), predispose many older patients in hospitals and nursing facility residents to falls, and subsequently cause them. However, the degree of individual fall risk and the etiology, or causes, of falls among older people varies considerably. Because of interindividual variability (e.g., differences in coexisting medical problems, their number and severity; the number, types, and dosages of medications used; the level of cognitive function and mobility capacity; design and structure of institutional environments), some people are at greater fall risk than others, and thus, the etiology of falls is different. Consequently, both the prediction of individual fall risk and the determination of fall etiology is difficult without a comprehensive systematic approach.

Terminology

Differential diagnosis	Distinguishing between two or more diseases with similar symptoms by systematically comparing their signs and symptoms
Hypoglycemia	Low blood sugar
Orthostatic hypotension	Lowered blood pressure that occurs on rising to an erect position
Proprioception	Muscle and joint sensations of body's position in space
Syncope	Fainting; temporary unconsciousness

The primary aim of the clinical assessment is to identify people who are at risk for falls and, in those with falls, to discover the causative factors. Once these factors have been identified, a clinical evaluation is performed in order to design preventive or interventional strategies to reduce fall risk. The steps involved in the fall and fall risk assessment are outlined in Figure 3-1.

Fall Assessment

A falling episode should be followed by an evaluation and treatment of physical injury, life-threatening medical conditions, or both that may have precipitated or followed the falling event. Any time a fall occurs, the patient or resident should not be moved or assisted in getting up from the floor until the possibility of injury has been eliminated. Also, any symptoms or signs of acute medical problems must be referred for medical attention immediately. Figure 3-2 is an injury and medical emergency checklist that nurses can use as a referral tool.

Once the patient or resident is medically stable, a history of the circumstances surrounding the fall should be taken to help determine the differential diagnosis. Taking a history is analogous to inquiring about any other medical symptom such as abdominal pain or chest

Step 1

Patient or resident has fallen: Proceed to Step 2. Patient or resident has not fallen: Proceed to Step 4.

Step 2

Evaluate for physical injury and/or acute medical problems. Treatment as indicated.

Step 3

Obtain fall history, circumstances of incident.

Step 4

Review fall risk factors (medical, psychological, functional histories).

Step 5

Obtain POEMS (see p. 50).

Step 6

Do physical examination.

Step 7

Obtain laboratory and diagnostic studies as indicated.

Step 8

List differential diagnosis of fall(s) and/or identified fall risk factors.

Step 9

Implement interventions to reduce fall risk.

Step 10

Monitor/follow-up to determine success of interventions.

Step 11

Repeat assessment if patient or resident continues to fall. If no falls, proceed to Step 12.

Step 12

Repeat fall risk assessment on a regular basis.

Figure 3-1. Steps involved in the fall and fall risk assessments.

pain. To discover the etiology, a history of the circumstances should be obtained, as should descriptive information on the duration, severity, and location of the discomfort. Taking a fall history consists of asking the person about any symptoms experienced at the time of the fall or those occurring prior to the fall (e.g., dizziness, heart palpitations, loss of consciousness or balance, legs giving away, trips or slips) and for a description of the activity the person was engaged in at the time of the fall. As older adults may have poor recollection of these events because of cognitive impairment, reports from nurses, other

Injury and Acute Medical Problem Checklist

Summon for medical assistance if patient/resident complains of

Difficulty moving arms or legs?	Yes	No
Pain/injury in arms, legs, or lower back?	Yes	No
Headache/head injury?	Yes	No
Confusion/lethargy?	Yes	No
Dizziness/lightheadedness?	Yes	No
Loss of consciousness?	Yes	No
Convulsions?	Yes	No
Chest pain/difficulty breathing?	Yes	No
Fast, slow, or irregular pulse rate?	Yes	No

If you suspect a hip or pelvic fracture (e.g., pain in hip, lower back, or groin area; extremity pain that worsens with movement), do not try to move the person.

Figure 3-2.

staff members, and family members who may have witnessed the fall can be helpful. In addition, the location, time (hour of the day) of the fall, and any injuries sustained should be documented.

Asking patients and residents to recount the circumstances of their falls provides valuable clues to the etiologies. For example, falls associated with rising from a bed or chair and experiencing symptoms of dizziness may point to orthostatic hypotension. An absence of symptoms may implicate the design, the height, or the stability of the bed or chair as a causative factor. If a person complains of tripping or slipping, the environment (e.g., hazardous ground surface camouflaged by poor lighting; wet floors, upended carpet edges or linoleum tiles) may be the precipitating cause, either by itself or in combination with an underlying gait disorder.

In addition, the history should include inquiry about previous falls and their circumstances. This inquiry helps to determine whether there is a pattern to the falls. The majority of people who fall repeatedly do so under similar circumstances. This kind of information, if not available from the patient or resident, may be gathered from a review of available past incident reports or medical records. It is equally important to solicit information about near-falls. Near-falls are events in which a person loses balance but manages to avert a fall to the ground by grabbing onto an environmental object such as the back of a chair, a headboard, or a table edge for support. (If the environmental object had not been available for support, the person probably would have suffered a fall to the ground.) Observational studies of older people residing in institutions have demonstrated that in the course of their daily activities, many frail individuals encounter an increased frequency of near-falls, which increases the risk of falling.[1]

Other questions that should be asked about previous falls include whether the person has experienced any physical injury or loss of self-confidence in performing activities, or, subsequently, has restricted his or her mobility in any way. A positive response to the latter may indicate a fear of subsequent falls.

A thorough history aimed at identifying the circumstances associated with falling represents the foundation of determining fall etiology because all subsequent evaluations are based, in part, on the information obtained. As such, the fall history (see Figure 3-3 for fall history components represented by the acronym SPLATT) can be in-

Symptoms experienced at time of fall(s)

Previous number of falls or near falls

Location of fall(s)

Activity engaged in at time of fall(s)

Time (hour of day) of fall(s)

Trauma (physical, psychological) associated with fall(s)

Figure 3-3. Fall history and the SPLATT.

corporated into existing hospital and nursing facility incident reports and thus becomes a standard part of any investigation of falls.

Fall Risk Assessment

The assessment of fall risk in older adult patients of hospitals and residents of nursing facilities begins with the identification of individual risk factors from the thorough history.

Identification of Individual Risk Factors

A thorough history can detect most people who are at high fall risk. The individual taking the history should inquire about the occurrence of falls during the previous 3 months and the circumstances surrounding the fall(s), and review the medical history for conditions and medications that place patients or residents at risk. In identifying individual fall risk factors, one should look for the following:

Visual impairment
Postural hypotension
Reduced lower-extremity strength
Impaired gait and balance
Impaired mobility
Use of ambulation assistive devices
Bladder dysfunction
Altered cognition
Sedatives, psychotropics, hypnotics, and antihypertensive drugs

These factors, particularly when they occur simultaneously, have been associated repeatedly with fall risk; attempts to ascertain their presence should be included in the risk assessment of patients and residents. Although these factors by themselves increase susceptibility to falls, their relationship as a true measure of fall risk is more accurately reflected by their effects on an individual's ability to ambulate and transfer safely and independently in the living environment. Any impairment in gait and balance that results from these factors is a strong predictor of fall risk. Therefore, a performance-oriented environmental mobility screen (POEMS), which evaluates how competently patients and residents execute a number of positional changes and movements during their daily activities, should be obtained.

Performance-Oriented Environmental Mobility Screen

POEMS constitutes the second step of the assessment of fall risk and is beneficial in identifying host-related situations and environmental conditions that cause dysmobility in people at fall risk. POEMS (forms are included in Appendix A) assesses the following performance items: balance maintained in sitting and rising from a chair, bed, and toilet; standing balance; ability to bend down from a standing position; and ability to ambulate in both the bedroom and bathroom. Transfer and ambulation maneuvers are tested with or without assistive devices as applicable. Testing the person's capacity to ambulate in different locations takes into account that the space limitations, ground surfaces, and illumination of the space are dissimilar and represent different risks. Individuals are scored on each task as being either normal (i.e., independent mobility) or impaired (i.e., person is unsteady during performance or unable to accomplish the task or perform the task safely). Any impaired execution indicates that the person is at fall risk.

Depending on the patient's or resident's state of health during time of admission and institutional stay, the sequence of POEMS maneuvers may be altered to accommodate the individual. In patients and residents who are ill, the length of the POEMS is determined by the individual's capacity to continue performing the maneuver safely. The list below suggests sequences for people who are ill and for people who are well.

- Illness
  - Transfer off bed
  - Stand after rising from bed (eyes open)
  - Stand with eyes closed
  - Stand in place (sternal nudge)
  - Bend down, pick up object
  - Walk about bedroom/bed
  - Walk to/about bathroom
  - Sit down/rise from toilet
  - Walk up/down hallway
  - Transfer onto bed
- Wellness
  - Sit down/rise from chair
  - Stand after rising from chair (eyes open)

Stand with eyes closed
Stand in place (sternal nudge)
Bend down, pick up object
Transfer onto/off bed
Walk about bedroom/bathroom
Sit down on/rise from toilet
Walk up/down hallway

POEMS is initiated in the older person's bedroom. The individual is asked to sit down and rise from a chair. The person doing the screening should observe the person's ability to complete the activity in a smooth and controlled movement, without loss of balance or the use of armrests. The chair should not tip or slide away and the person's feet should not slide but rest flat on the floor (Figure 3-4). Next, the person should be instructed to rise from the chair and remain standing in place for approximately 30 seconds. The person doing the screening should observe whether the person is able to stand without loss of balance or support from the chair to maintain balance (Figure 3-5). The person should be asked to participate in the Romberg test, which assesses proprioceptive function: He or she should remain standing with eyes closed, arms placed at the sides, and feet planted approximately 3 inches apart. Inability to maintain balance, as demonstrated by increased postural sway or grabbing environmental furnishings for support, indicates an abnormality (Figure 3-6).

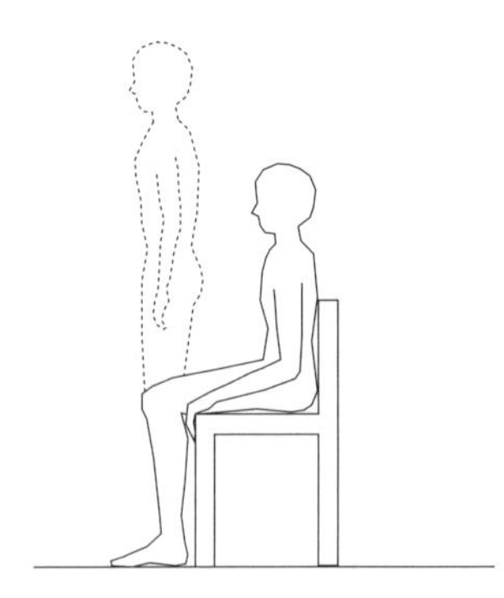

Figure 3-4. Chair transfer.

A sternal push test should be performed by the examiner with the person still standing with his or her eyes open. The push test consists of nudging the person's sternum lightly with the fingers while applying enough force to induce balance displacement (Figure 3-7). This maneuver tests postural competence in response to loss of balance. The normal reaction is to stretch the arms forward, away from the body, and to take one or two steps backward (Figure 3-8). Both movements represent the body's ability to compensate for sudden balance shifts. The inability to maintain balance (e.g., a fall backward) signifies an

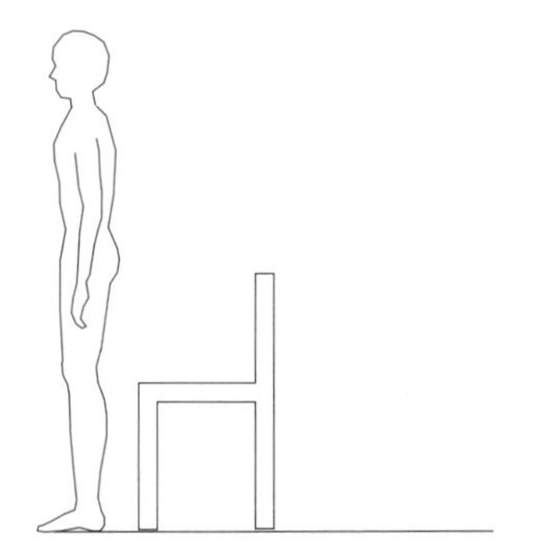

Figure 3-5. Immediate standing balance.

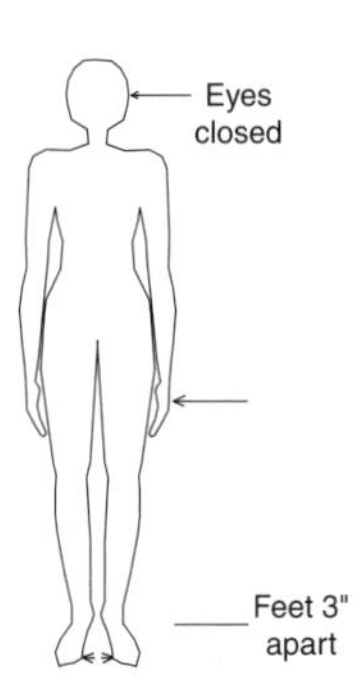

Figure 3-6. Romberg test.

abnormality (Figure 3-9). During these postural tests, it is prudent for another staff member to be positioned behind the person in the event of a fall. In extremely frail individuals or in those whose impaired balance recovery is obvious from appearances, the sternal push test may be omitted for safety reasons.

Following the body displacement tests, the person should be asked to bend from a normal standing position as if to retrieve an object from the floor. The examiner should observe whether the person is steady, able to maintain balance without holding onto furnishings for support (Figure 3-10). Assessing the person's reaching activities, such as obtaining clothing from closets and other storage areas used by the individual, are examined in a similar fashion.

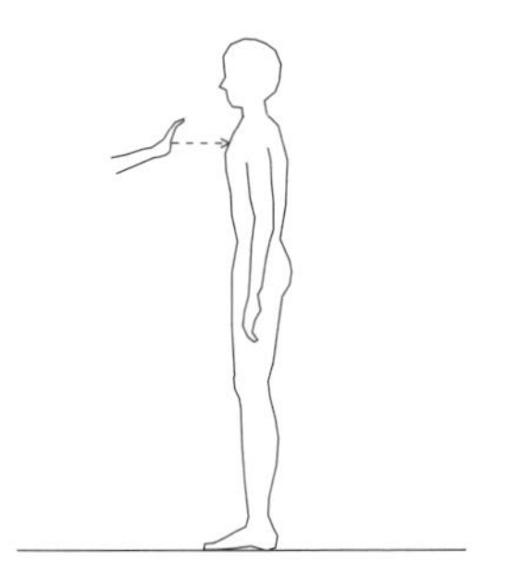

Figure 3-7. Sternal push test.

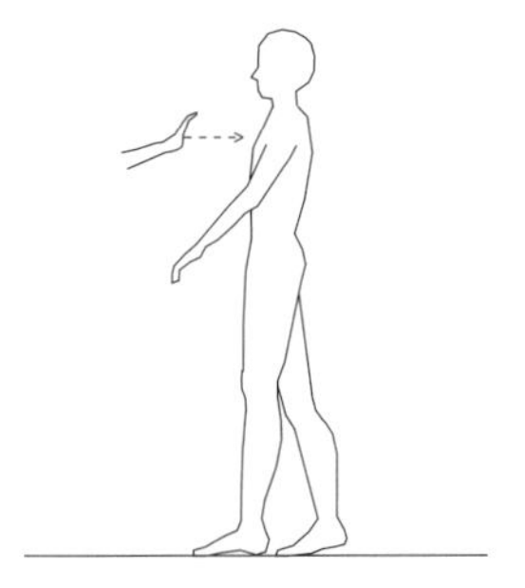

Figure 3-8. A normal reaction to body displacement.

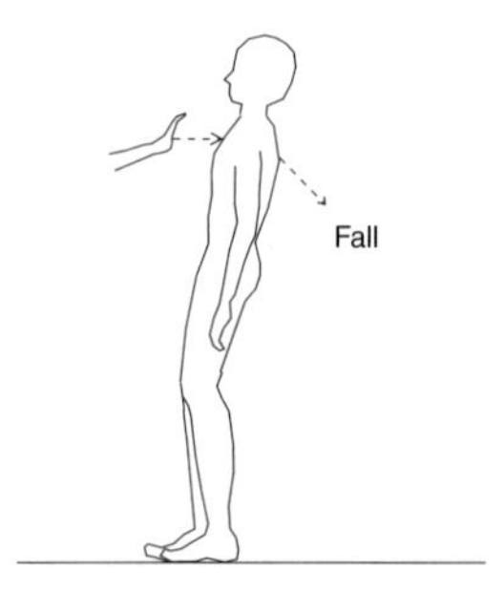

Figure 3-9. An abnormal reaction to body displacement.

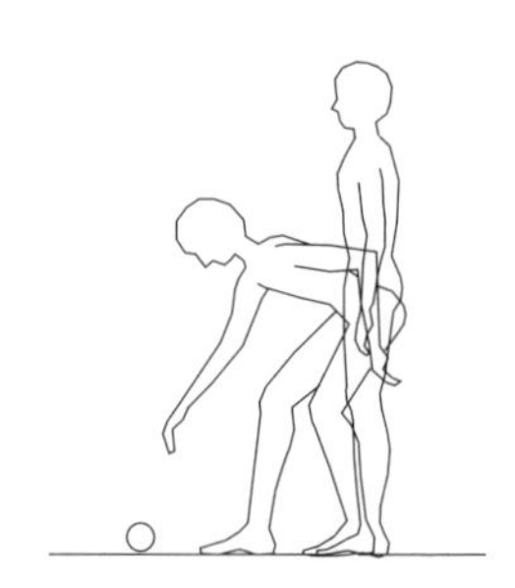

Figure 3-10. Bending-down performance.

Moving to the bed, the person should be asked to transfer onto and off it. The person's ability to perform this maneuver smoothly and controlled without loss of balance or need for arm support to maintain sitting balance on the mattress should be observed and rated. Also, the bed should remain steady (i.e., without moving or sliding away). The older person's feet should rest flat on the floor in the seated position (Figure 3-11).

The next test is that of ambulation ability. The person should be asked to walk about and turn around, first in the bedroom and then in the bathroom using the ambulation device, if applicable. The examiner should observe the person's gait and balance, whether the gait is continuous, whether it occurs without hesitation or excessive deviation

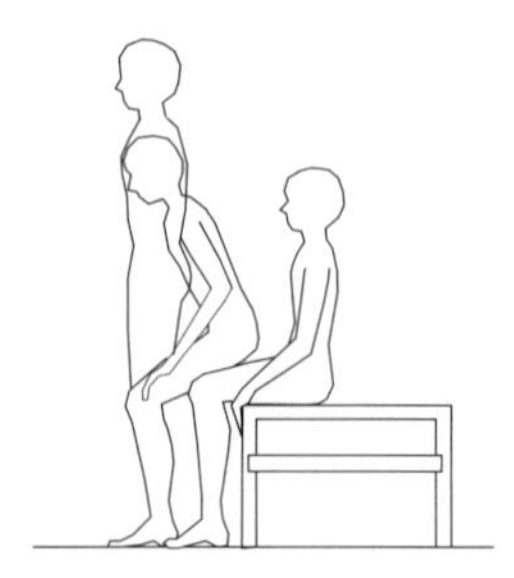

Figure 3-11. Bed transfer.

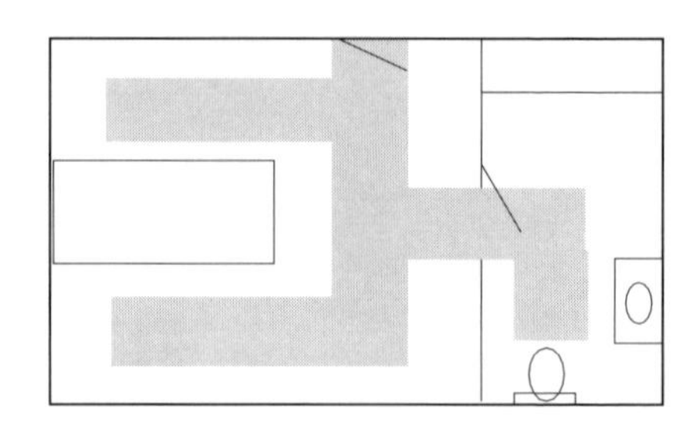

Figure 3-12. Common environmental walking routes are reflected by the shaded areas. A person should be able to use his or her ambulation device safely in all areas.

from side to side, whether both feet clear the surface of the floor, whether any staggering or losing balance and grabbing environmental surfaces (e.g., bed, chair backs, sink edge, walls) for support take place, and whether the ambulation device is used safely and fits into spaces (e.g., both sides of the bed, in the bathroom) (Figure 3-12).

Toilet transfer is the next test in POEMS. The person should be asked to transfer onto and off the toilet. As with other tests, the person should be observed for his or her ability to perform this activity in a smooth, controlled movement, without loss of balance or the need to hold onto the sink edge or grab bars for support (Figure 3-13). Finally, the person should walk from the bedroom and down the hallway to the nurses' station and other locations, such as the dining room. The person should be observed for his or her ability to walk without gait and balance difficulties or fatigue.

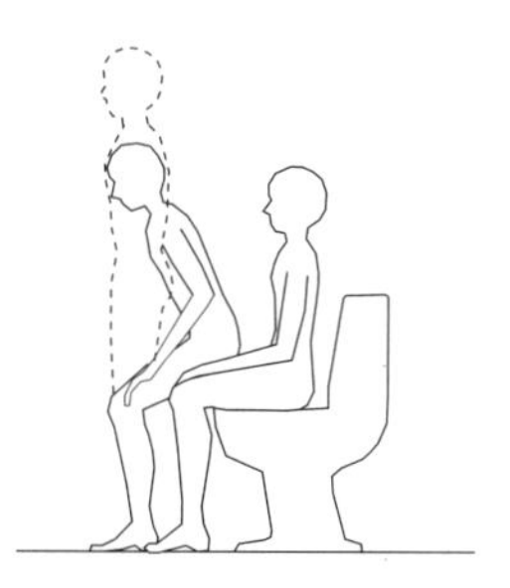

Figure 3-13. Toilet transfer.

If POEMS is normal (i.e., the patient or resident is able to perform the maneuvers independently), the person is at low fall risk. However, any impairment in execution of a task indicates the presence of underlying intrinsic and/or extrinsic factors (Table 3-1) that place the individual at fall risk.

POEMS has several advantages: It is easy to understand and administer by nurses and nursing assistants in both hospital and nursing facility settings. In general, it takes no longer than 10 minutes to complete, even with the frailest people. In addition to detecting mobility dysfunction, POEMS also can be used to help design rehabilitative and environmental interventions and to monitor clinical changes or outcomes (e.g., the effects of medical conditions, medications, environmental influences) over time.

Optimally, the fall risk assessment should be completed when people are first admitted to the hospital or nursing facility, as the risk of falling is greatest during the first few days of institutional stay. However, completing the assessment may not always be feasible or practical, particularly in an acute care hospital. On admission to an acute care facility, patients may be injured (e.g., hip fracture) or severely ill. Often, people with rapidly fluctuating medical conditions are maintained by bed rest. In these instances risk assessment is best admin-

Table 3-1. POEMS differential diagnoses

Impaired maneuver	Intrinsic factors	Extrinsic factors
Chair, bed and toilet transfers	Parkinsonism Arthritis Deconditioning Adverse drug effect	Poor chair, bed, or toilet design
Standing balance	Postural hypotension Vestibular dysfunction Adverse drug effects	
Romberg test	Proprioceptive dysfunction Adverse drug effects	Poor illumination Overly absorptive footwear, carpeting, or both
Sternal push	Parkinsonism Normal pressure hydrocephalus Adverse drug effects	
Bending down	Central nervous system dysfunction Adverse drug effects	
Walking/turning	Foot disorders Parkinsonism Hemiparesis Sensory dysfunction Adverse drug effects	Improper footwear Improper size/use of ambulation device Hazardous ground surfaces

istered after any acute problem or condition is treated and stabilized or at a time when the patient is permitted to assume an independent level of function. In both hospitals and nursing facilities, risk should be reassessed whenever the person's medical condition, medication regimen (e.g., the addition or subtraction of drugs, dosage modifications), and functional status change.

Other Assessment Tools

In nursing facilities and certain hospital units, such as psychiatric wards, where people reside for prolonged periods of time, risk assessment, particularly POEMS, should be repeated at established intervals—approximately every 3–6 months. POEMS can be incorporated into the Minimum Data Set 2.0 (MDS 2.0; Long-Term Care Facility Resident Assessment Instrument) in nursing facilities as follows:

Full Assessment Form
Section G: Physical Functioning and Structural Problems
- Bed mobility
- Transfer
- Walk in room
- Walk in corridor
- Locomotion on unit
- Toilet use
- Test for balance
- Modes of locomotion
- Modes of transfer
- Change in ADL function

MDS Quarterly Assessment Form
Section G1: ADL Performance
- Bed mobility
- Walk in room
- Walk in corridor
- Toilet use
- Modes of transfer

Resident Assessment Protocols
- Failure to Thrive (ADLs)
- Activities of Daily Living—Functional Rehabilitation Potential
- Falls
- Psychotropic Drug-Related Side Effects (unsteady gait/balance)

Physical Restraints (risk of falls)

The aim of this combination is to identify people with gradually deteriorating health conditions because any decline in mobility can indicate an early sign of disease and fall risk.

A fall risk checklist is presented in Figure 3-14, which can be used to help identify and record individual risk factors. In addition, the checklist can be incorporated into existing institutional examination

Fall Risk Checklist

Risk Factors

- ❏ Previous falls
- ❏ Visual impairment
- ❏ Postural hypotension
- ❏ Balance disorder
- ❏ Cognitive impairment (depression, dementia, poor judgment)
- ❏ Gait disorder
- ❏ Lower extremity weakness
- ❏ Arthritis (knee, hips)
- ❏ Medications (psychotropics, sedatives, hypnotics, antihypertensives)
- ❏ Bladder dysfunction (frequency, urgency, nocturia, incontinence)

Describe Circumstances of Falls

Symptoms:

Location:

Time of day:

Activity:

Trauma:

(continued)

Figure 3-14. Fall risk checklist.

Fall Risk Checklist (continued)

Mobility

Location	Maneuver	Independent	Impaired
Bedroom	Chair transfers		
	Sitting	❑	❑
	Rising	❑	❑
	Standing balance	❑	❑
	Immediate	❑	❑
	Romberg test	❑	❑
	Sternal push test	❑	❑
	Bending-down balance	❑	❑
	Bed transfer		
	Sitting	❑	❑
	Rising	❑	❑
	Ambulation		
	Straight path	❑	❑
	Turning	❑	❑
Bathroom	Toilet transfers		
	Sitting	❑	❑
	Rising	❑	❑
	Ambulation		
	Straight path	❑	❑
	Turning	❑	❑
	Other	❑	❑
		❑	❑
		❑	❑
		❑	❑

Figure 3-14.

forms. medical and nursing records, and incident reports. Once a patient or resident is identified as being at fall risk, all staff must be alerted. A number of measures have been used by nursing staff to recognize individuals at risk: application of brightly colored stickers placed on the medical and nursing charts, bedroom door, and bedside, and distinctively colored wrist-identification bands or slippers to be worn by the person at risk.

Several hospitals and nursing facilities have developed standard fall risk assessment tools that predict the susceptibility to falls (see Bibliography). The sources of data used to develop these risk profiles vary greatly (e.g., incident report data, literature reviews of risk factors, staff experiences). A number of potential problems with these risk assessment tools have been identified. Staff members have varied definitions of a fall they report; some institutions may require only those falls with physical injury to be reported; profiles developed from the literature are often skewed toward characteristics of a particular institution, hospital, or nursing facility; and within each institution, specific factors derived from specialized units (e.g., oncology, orthopedic, surgery, psychiatric, rehabilitation, neurology, stroke; dementia-specific care unit) may not apply to different institutions or settings.

Staffing patterns and environmental designs also may affect fall risk; indeed, in some instances they may constitute a greater determinant of risk than the characteristics of patients or residents by themselves. The most effective procedure is to examine the risk assessment tools available and choose several that seem to reflect the particular population of the facility. Each procedure should be used in a pilot program within hospital units and nursing facility floors that have a high incidence of falls. Their success is measured by assessing a group of people who have experienced falls and comparing them with a group of people without falls. Using the tool in this way should determine whether it is sensitive enough to differentiate fall risk. Questions that should be answered while using the tool are does the tool work? Does it accurately identify patients and residents at risk for falling? Is the tool practical? Do nurses find the instrument user-friendly for routine use? Being able to accurately identify patients and residents at risk on a regular basis enables resources (e.g. nursing and rehabilitative staff, safety equipment, assistive devices) to be targeted toward prevention.

Clinical Evaluation

Once the falls and fall risk assessments have been completed, multiple fall etiologies and risk factors may be identified via clinical evaluation. The primary aim of the clinical evaluation is twofold: First, in people with a fall or falls, it isolates a specific cause; in people with identifiable risk factors, it uncovers the presence of remedial or modifiable factors. Second, the clinical evaluation determines in both groups the existence of any new risk factors that may not have been detected previously. Although, in general, the clinical evaluation is the province of physicians, allied health professionals (e.g., physician's assistants, nurse practitioners, clinicians) are equally adept in assessment techniques. The services of these professionals are useful, particularly in the nursing facility, where the presence of physicians is rare.

The clinical evaluation of patients and residents with falls begins with a review of the medical records, current medical problems, and medications. This review may provide important clues to the factors contributing to falls. For example, if a person experiences dizziness prior to a fall and records indicate the recent addition of a diuretic, the association of the two factors may indicate that the fall has been caused by an adverse medication effect. Similarly, if a person has arthritis of the knees and falls while transferring from a chair, the arthritis may be partially responsible for the fall.

Once the person's historical information is compiled, a POEMS should be obtained. As in people at fall risk, the value of POEMS for people who have fallen lies in isolating organ systems and environmental problems that may provide insight into the possible etiology of the fall. The next step is to perform a physical examination that includes comprehensive cognitive, neurological, musculoskeletal, and cardiac evaluations. Information gathered from the falls/fall-risk assessments and POEMS can serve as a focus for the physical examination. For example, if the fall history reveals that a fall occurred in association with dizziness and changes in position and POEMS demonstrates a loss of balance, unsteadiness, and/or the complaint of dizziness on immediate standing, postural changes in blood pressure must be assessed to rule out or confirm orthostatic hypotension. Similarly, if the person demonstrates difficulty with chair or bed transferring during POEMS, the physical examination should concentrate on evaluating the musculoskeletal system for reduced muscle strength. Not only will any abnormality discovered during the physical examination help to identify the cause of falls and modifiable risk factors but other, not-directly-related findings, which may increase the risk of subsequent falls, may be detected.

Once the physical examination has been completed, the next step is to perform laboratory and diagnostic studies. The extent of testing is dictated by the information gathered from all previous evaluations.

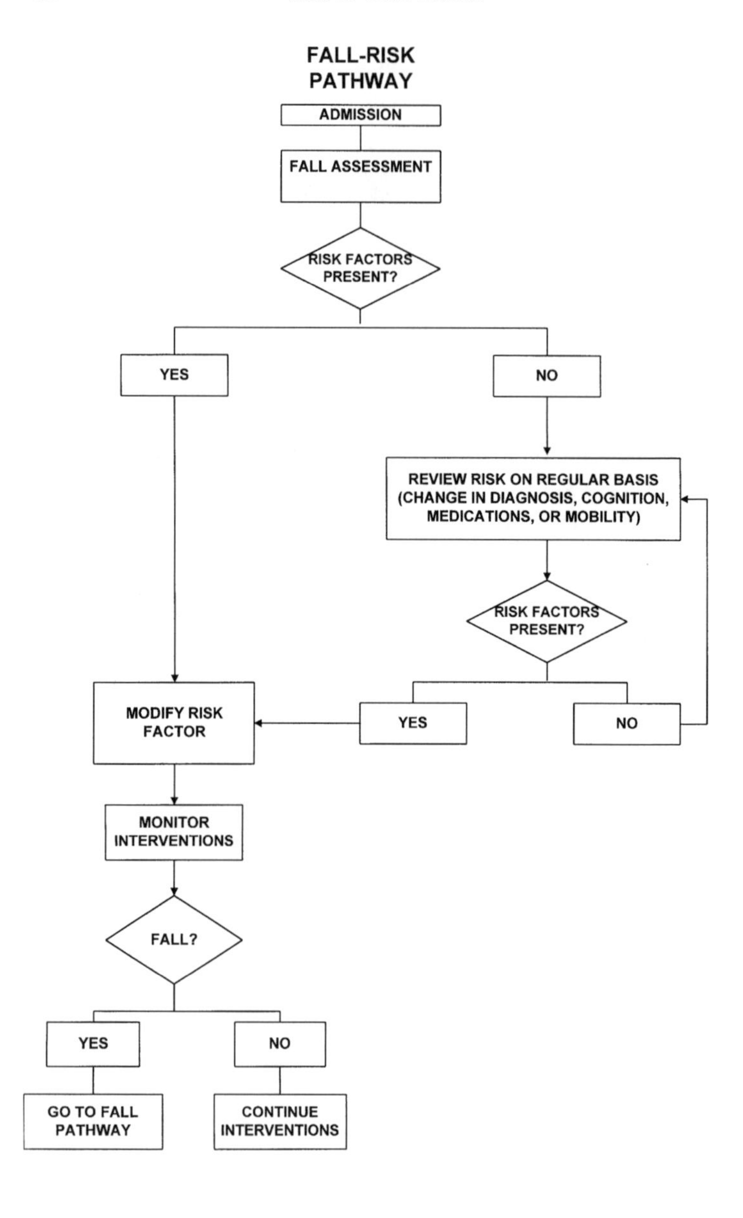

Figure 3-15. The fall-risk assessment pathway should be repeated regularly to identify new or changing risk factors.

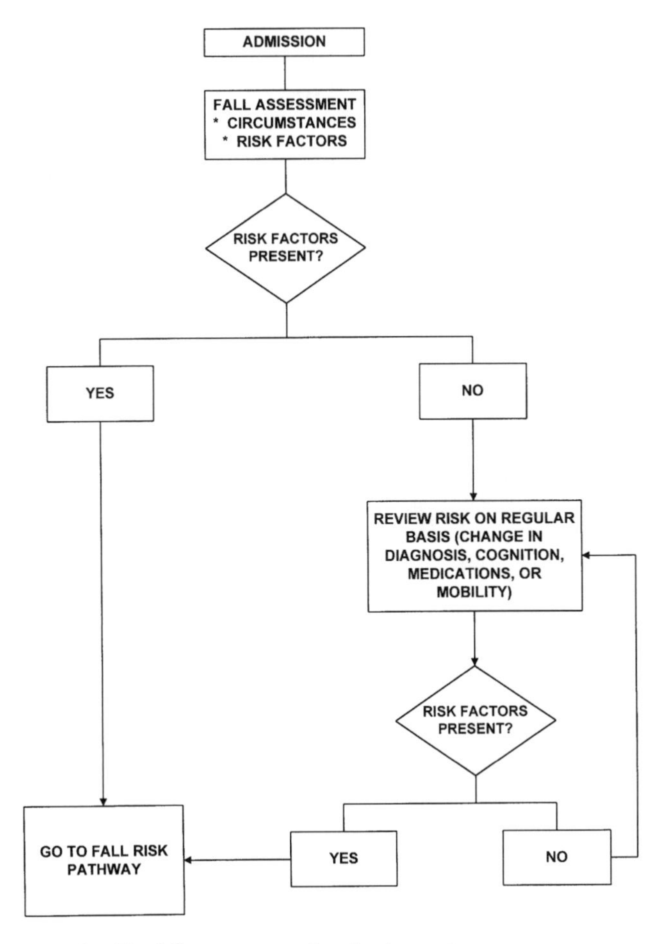

Figure 3-16. The fall assessment and evaluation pathway.

For example, if the physical examination confirms the presence of orthostatic hypotension, blood and stool testing for volume-depleted states such as dehydration, blood loss, and anemia must be ordered. If the person is diabetic and the history suggests falls resulting from hypoglycemia, a blood glucose test should be obtained. If the fall is associated with a syncopal episode and the physical examination reveals an irregular pulse rate, an electrocardiogram and possibly a Holter monitoring study should be considered. A history of bladder dysfunction demands urine and blood tests and urodynamic studies to search for underlying causes. Similarly, manifestations of lower-extremity weakness on physical examination indicates the need for tests that may explain the etiology.

After all evaluations are complete, a list of intrinsic or extrinsic (or both) factors responsible for fall risk or falls can be compiled. From the list(s), interventions to reduce the risk of subsequent falls should follow (see Chapter 4). Follow-up ensures that the intervention strategies employed are effective. Repeat the fall risk assessment on a regular basis to identify new or changing risk factors (Figure 3-15). If the person continues to fall, repeat the fall assessment and evaluation (Figure 3-16). Some factor may have been missed or overlooked from previous evaluations or the person may have developed an additional condition that causes falls. It is important to remember that falls and fall risk are not fixed or static processes, but rather are dynamic events, and the causes can change as often as do the person's medical conditions and environmental surroundings.

NOTES

[1]Connell, B.R., & Wolf, S.L. (1993). Patterns of naturally occurring falls among frail nursing home residents. *Gerontologist*, 33(Special Issue), 58.

chapter four

Preventive Strategies to Reduce Fall Risk

The goal of fall prevention strategies is to design interventions that minimize fall risk by ameliorating or eliminating contributing factors while maintaining or improving patients' and residents' mobility. Potential preventive strategies are based on known risk factors and postulated causes of falls and can be classified as medical, rehabilitative, and environmental. In most cases management of people at fall risk includes components derived from each category. Although little direct evidence exists on the effectiveness of any one of these particular approaches in preventing falls, common sense suggests that they are promising and should be attempted. A description of these measures designed to prevent or reduce the incidence of falls, which can be used by hospital and nursing facility staff along with an elaboration of fall prevention programs developed in institutional settings, follows.

Medical Strategies

The importance of identifying patients and residents at fall risk and those with falls and following up with a clinical evaluation of each to identify modifiable factors cannot be overemphasized. Each factor may represent a sign or symptom of an underlying disease or medication effect that requires a clinician's attention in order to rule out reversible acute problems, identify chronic medical conditions that may contribute, and treat each appropriately. Of equal importance is the assessment of medications. All drugs should be reviewed carefully in terms of their risks and benefits. Dosages should be examined with an eye toward reduction when possible. Any combination of drugs should be monitored on a regular basis for potential drug interactions. In particular, drugs that affect mobility or increase fall risk such as sedatives, hypnotics, and psychoactives should be scrutinized routinely.

As a general rule, medications in older people should be initiated at their lowest effective dose, increased slowly while monitoring for side effects and clinical efficacy, maintained at the lowest possible dose, and discontinued when no longer effective. For patients and residents with osteoporosis who are at risk for injurious falls, consideration of drug treatment (e.g., calcium supplements and medications that reduce bone loss) to modify the risk of hip and other fractures is advised.

Rehabilitative Strategies

Patients and residents who fail to respond or improve with medical treatment and continue to remain at fall risk, particularly those with chronic neuromuscular disorders, may respond to a number of rehabilitative strategies. These strategies include engaging in exercise therapy, wearing proper footwear, employing hip-protective pads, and using appropriate ambulation devices to assist with mobility.

Exercise

People with impaired muscular strength and altered gait and balance, or the consequences of underlying medical conditions, deconditioning, or both, may benefit from low-intensity leg strengthening and weight-bearing exercises as well as gait, balance, and transfer training generally provided by physiatrists and physical therapists. These kinds of exercise and training programs are designed to restore and maintain muscle strength and coordination, bone mass, joint flexibility and movement, vestibular and proprioceptive function, and postural control reflexes, as well as teach individuals effective bed, chair, and toilet transfer techniques. In addition, a variety of exercise programs that nurses and nursing assistants can easily perform on their own to help maintain patient and resident mobility is found below. Figure 4-1 illustrates a set of simple exercises designed to maintain or improve mobility. These exercises can be performed by staff either at the person's bedside or in a group setting, depending on the institution. These exercises should be started gradually and be done twice daily. The facilitator should work at the patient's or resident's own pace and level

Daily Floor Ambulation Program

Ambulatory patients or residents are encouraged to walk at least 3 times daily, or 30–45 minutes a day as tolerated, to the dining room, planned activities, and so forth. Assistance with ambulation is provided for individuals with poor gait and balance and/or fear of falling. The use of wheelchairs is discouraged.

"Walkers Group"

Ambulatory patients or residents are encouraged to walk daily from bed to bathroom, from bedroom to nurses' station, from bedroom to the end of the hallway, from one end of the hallway to the other end, and so forth, with set goals determined by physical condition. Rewards are given for achieving each goal.

Wheelchair Walking Program

Patients or residents are encouraged to "walk" with their chairs—move their wheelchair along by using their legs. This exercise helps them to maintain effective and safe transfers and improves lower extremity function. Removing the footrests discourages their use.

Mobility Program

Patients or residents are encouraged to ambulate and/or stand at least three times daily and to walk to the activity room for group exercises and meals daily. Patients, residents, and/or their caregivers are taught active and passive range of motion exercises, weight-bearing exercises, and resistive and aerobic exercises.

Exercise 1: Chair Rise/Sit (improves lower-extremity strength and joint motion)

Ask the patient or resident to stand up from a stable chair and then sit down. If necessary, the patient or resident should use the armrest of the chair for support. 8–10 reps, as tolerated.

Exercise 2: Modified Sit-Up (improves lower-extremity strength and joint motion)

Ask the patient or resident to lift each leg from the knee. 6–8 reps, as tolerated.

Exercise 3: Standing Knee Bend (improves lower-extremity strength and balance)

Ask the patient or resident to lift leg, bend, and straighten at knee. Alternate right and left legs. 10 reps, as tolerated.

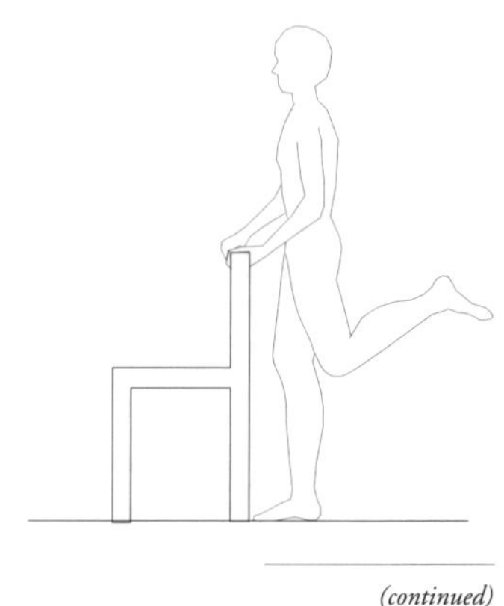

(continued)

Figure 4-1. Flexibility and balance exercise program.

Exercise 4: Shoulder Shrug (improves upper-extremity range of motion)

Ask the patient or resident to sit up or stand up straight, shrug the shoulders up high, and release. 10 reps, as tolerated.

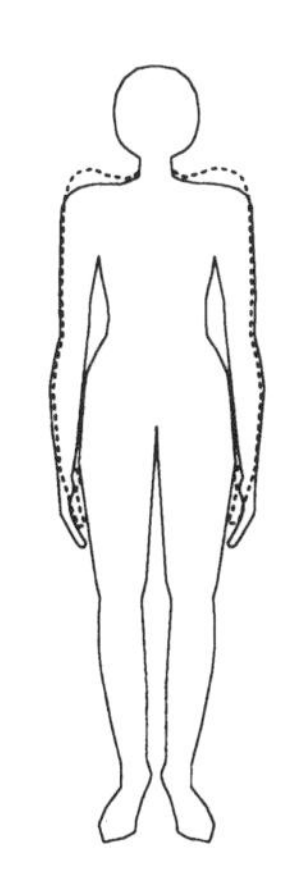

Exercise 5: Arm Circles (improves upper-extremity range of motion)

Ask the patient or resident to sit up or stand up straight. With each arm make a circle, which gradually increases to become as large as possible. Begin the exercise with the arms 6 inches from sides and circle arms upward and down again. Each circle, 20 seconds; 2 reps, as tolerated.

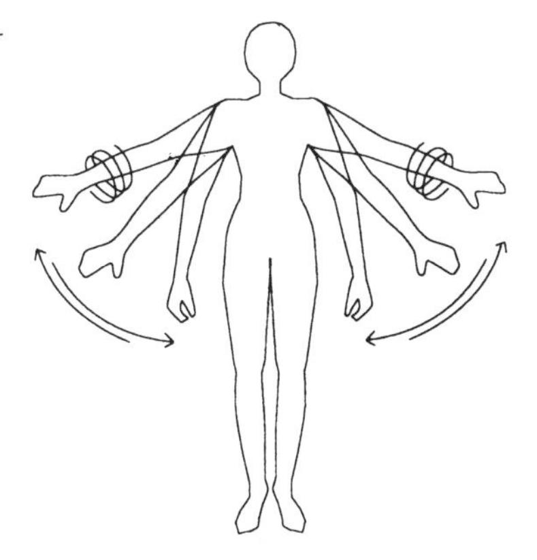

Exercise 6: Ankle Pumps (improves ankle strength and balance)

Ask the patient or resident to lift up body on tiptoes and lower body back down while holding on to the back of a stable chair. This exercise may be done in a chair if the patient or resident has poor balance: Ask the individual to lift up heels and stand on tiptoes and lower the heels back down again. 15 reps, as tolerated.

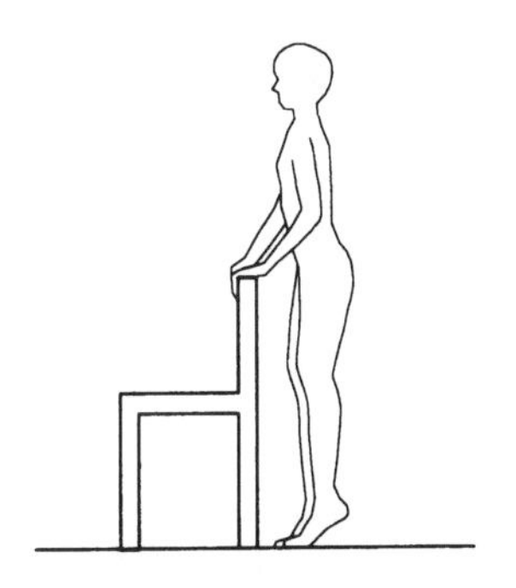

Figure 4-1.

of stability. (Strength building can be intensified by adding 1- to 2-pound weights to Exercises 2 and 3.) For most patients and residents, these exercise therapy programs pose a minimal risk of adverse effects (i.e., injury), and they may be effective in combating impaired mobility and decreasing the risk of falls and injury.

A growing body of evidence suggests that older people respond to exercise therapy, even those who are very old and frail. Exercise can enhance the functioning of other organ systems involved in mobility endurance, such as cardiovascular and pulmonary performance. In addition, by building patients' and residents' self-confidence in performing activities, fear of falling or instability may be reduced. Because these individuals may be susceptible to falls and injury, caution is advised—a renewed sense of confidence and ability to execute mobility tasks may lead them to attempt activities that exceed their capabilities. This possibility should not dissuade staff from encouraging patient and resident independence in mobility, however. Instead, individuals should receive assistance at the beginning of such a program and the assistance should continue until the individual can participate in the activities safely and independently.

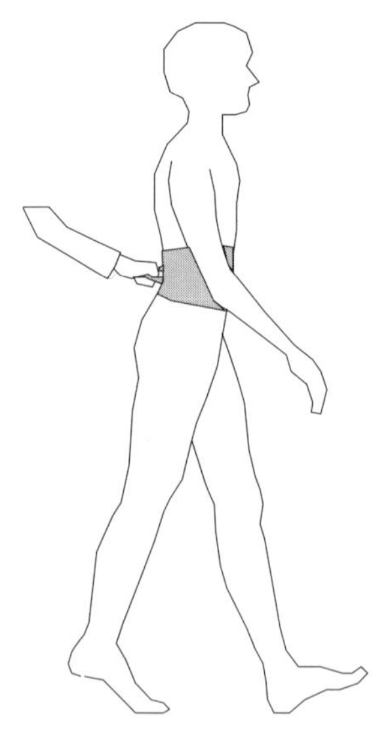

Figure 4-2. Assisted ambulation using a gait belt.

For people who fall, mobility should be encouraged as soon as possible in order to avoid the consequences of immobility. If patients or residents require assistance with walking, nursing staff can make use of a gait belt (Figure 4-2). The belt serves as a ready "handle" to grasp in the event that the older person begins to fall. Staff should hold on to the belt handles or the tail strap with one hand and, with the other hand, hold on to the person's shoulder, which helps to control balance if the older person falls forward or backward. If the patient or resident does lose balance, staff should maintain normal posture (i.e., do not bend over): The knees should be bent, with the feet spaced 12 inches apart. The person should be pulled gently toward the staff member or his or her descent to the ground controlled gently. Some staff and even the older person may find that a gait belt provides added security. To assist an individual walking without a cane, the staff member should position him- or herself in back and slightly to the side of the individual. If the individual uses a cane or hemiwalker, the staff member should stand on the opposite side of the device. To ensure safety, the patient or resident should never be pushed beyond safe limits—the activity should be stopped if the individual complains of fatigue or if gait and balance become unsafe; it is also a good idea to consult with a physical therapist on proper techniques for assisted walking.

Footwear

All footwear—shoes and slippers worn by patients and residents—should fit properly and have slip-resistant soles. If foot problems such as hammertoes, bunions, calluses, and nail disorders prohibit the wearing of proper-size shoes, individuals should be referred for podiatric care. To accommodate foot problems, individuals may be prescribed special therapeutic footwear (i.e., "Frankenstein" shoes). Some frail older people may experience difficulty walking in this type of shoe, which can increase fall risk. The shoes are somewhat heavy to wear, and, as a result, the person may shuffle when walking, which can lead to tripping. Cutting out the toe box of the shoes may be a good alternative to therapeutic footwear, which interferes with safe walking.

Shoes and slippers with rubber or crepe soles provide adequate slip resistance on linoleum floors. Socks with nonskid tread on the soles (Figure 4-3) are a good choice, particularly for people who make nocturnal bathroom trips. However, for some individuals, such as those with a shuffling gait or poor steppage height (i.e., inability to pick up the feet an adequate distance from the floor), slip-resistant soles may interfere with safe ambulation because the soles adhere to ground surfaces. In particular, disposable foam "hospital slippers" and sneakers or running shoes with thick rubber soles can adhere to the ground surface when an individual is walking in them. For such individuals, footwear with leather-type soles that promotes gliding

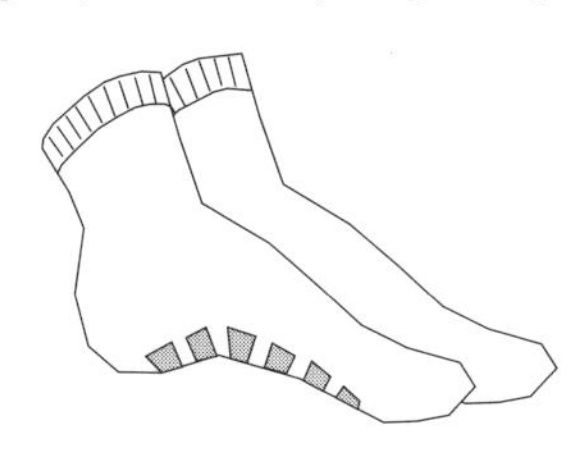

Figure 4-3. Socks with nonskid tread soles.

on linoleum and carpeted floor surfaces may be a better choice. In institutional settings having a mixture of floor surfaces (i.e., both linoleum and carpeting), however, a certain amount of caution in the selection of soles is suggested. For some older people, footwear with smooth soles (lack of traction) can facilitate walking on carpeted surfaces but promote slipping when walking on linoleum-covered surfaces.

Footwear with thick, soft soles may interfere with proprioceptive feedback (i.e., inability to "feel" the ground while walking), resulting in a loss of balance. Wearing thin, hard rubber–sole shoes (e.g., boat shoes, Topsiders) can help a person preserve his or her balance. The best way to evaluate the adequacy of the sole surface of footwear is to observe patients and residents as they walk on different floor surfaces in their environment to see whether their footwear interferes with safe ambulation.

High-heeled shoes should be avoided because they narrow a person's standing and walking base of support, which can lead to a loss of balance. Footwear with low, broad heels are a better choice and should be encouraged. These shoes are better suited for safe walking and balance. However, if the patient or resident insists on wearing high heels, either out of vanity or because of a real need—high heels worn over a long period of time cause a shortening of the Achilles tendon, which then necessitates their use—staff should encourage the wearing of shoes with wedge heels (Figure 4-4). Wedge heels provide a better base of support than ordinary high-heeled shoes, and they are less likely to catch on an elevated floor surface, such as upended carpet, linoleum tile edges, or door thresholds.

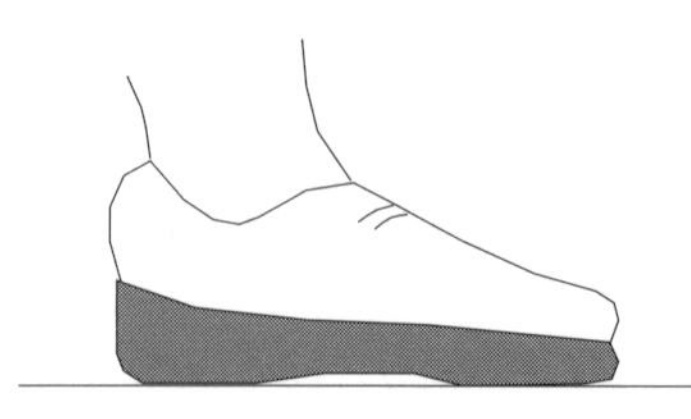

Figure 4-4. Shoes with wedge heels.

Hip-Padding Systems

More than 90% of hip fractures in older people are related to direct trauma against a hard ground surface following a fall. Hip-padding systems (Figure 4-5) are a strategy designed to act as shock absorbers around the hip (i.e., providing a cushion between the hip bone and impact surface), diverting the direct impact of a fall away from the bone, which helps to reduce the risk of a hip fracture. Two types of hip-padding systems are available in the United States, HipSaver and Hip-Guard; several other systems are being marketed in Europe.[1] Three different types of hip-padding systems are available:

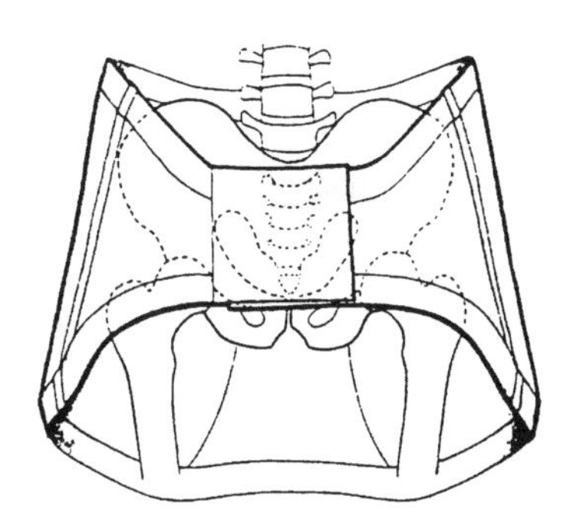

Figure 4-5. Example of a hip padding system (Hip-Guard). (Illustration reproduced with the permission of Prevent-Wise, Inc.)

1. Thin, elliptical plastic shields either sewn into specially designed undergarments or placed into pockets inside an ordinary pair of underwear; the shields are positioned to cover the hip bone
2. Two shock-absorbent foam pads inserted into a lightweight wraparound garment that is worn under outer clothing and over underwear; Velcro closures are used to allow for easy application and removal of the system
3. Adhesive pads made of flexible cork that fix directly to the skin over the hip area; the pads are designed to be left in place for several days

Hip-padding systems can be a significant factor in preventing hip fractures and have demonstrated benefits for both nursing facility residents and hospital patients.[2,3] However, questions remain as to who should wear hip pads, how to convince individuals to wear them, and what kinds of hip pads are the most effective.

Approximately 50%–80% of older people comply with hip protectors, wearing them regularly. Compliance is higher in individuals who are cognitively intact and in people who have recently experienced an injurious fall. A fear of falling improves the person's initial acceptance of hip protectors, perhaps by offering psychological benefit to him or her. Therefore, hip-padding systems may be most helpful as a preventive strategy against hip fractures in select groups of patients and residents such as those at risk for further hip fracture and those with a fear of falling or injury.

Individuals' noncompliance with wearing hip pads seems to be twofold: either initial rejection—the person does not want to wear hip pads—or later rejection—the person initially accepts wearing hip pads, but subsequently refuses to wear them. Several factors are associated with noncompliance, which include altered cognitive status and wearability.

Altered Cognitive Status

Patients and residents with dementia may lack the capacity to comprehend or recognize the need for hip protectors or they may become agitated while wearing the pads, forcing their removal. It is important to remember that not all people with dementia think about or respond to situations similarly; thus, some individuals reject hip pads or become disturbed by their presence, whereas other people accept and use hip protectors without complaint. In general, people with severe dementia are more tolerant of hip pads than are individuals with mild to moderate dementia. Because people with dementia are at significant risk for falling (e.g., by participating in hazardous activities, by not asking for assistance with activities; people with dementia tend to develop small-stepped gaits) and fracturing their hips, attempts to provide hip protectors in people with mild to moderate dementia should not be abandoned. Some patients and residents, especially those with dementia, may need to have the purpose of the hip protector explained to them each time it is applied in order to circumvent agitation.

Wearability

Some older individuals complain that hip protectors are uncomfortable to wear, that they are too bulky when sitting in chairs or while sleeping in bed, that they are too hot or tight to wear under clothing, and that they are too difficult to remove in readiness for toileting. Staff members sometimes complain that hip protectors are difficult to care for, particularly in people who are incontinent. Alternatives that increase compliance include

1. Selecting times when hip protectors are worn (e.g., days when individuals feel more unsteady) or not worn (e.g., dur-

ing sleep, although nocturia, or excessive urination at night, is a risk factor for falls)

2. Asking individuals to wear pants and dresses that are a few sizes larger than usual (to accommodate hip pads)
3. Providing soft-seated chairs, which may be more comfortable for people to sit in

Studies assessing the effectiveness of the different hip-padding systems in reducing hip fractures and increasing wearability are in progress. It is, therefore, too early to recommend any hip-padding system over the others with certainty. However, because sometimes the point of impact following a fall is not directly on the hip but on the buttock, the foam-padding system, which wraps around the pelvis, may offer more protection than the plastic shield system. The wraparound foam-padding system may protect against hip fracture in frail individuals with osteoporosis and poor balance who are constantly bumping against hard surfaces, such as walls and table edges. In addition, staff may find the foam-padding system easier to use in people who are incontinent because they can be used in conjunction with adult incontinence pads. If hip-padding systems are used, the possibility of sustaining a hip fracture cannot be excluded. Therefore, hip protectors alone cannot be relied on in the prevention of fractures, but must be used in conjunction with other preventive efforts.

Ambulation Devices

Ambulation devices, such as canes or walkers, are designed to improve gait and balance and to decrease the risk of falls. They work by creating greater stability, which increases an individual's standing and walking base of support because they provide an additional point(s) of ground contact (Figure 4-6). Ambulation devices furnish proprioceptive feedback through the handles and reduce the load on weight-bearing joints, such as hips and knees. Also, devices provide individuals with visual physical support, which instills confidence in them during ambulation, helping to reduce their fear of instability and falls.

The choice of a cane, whether single- or multistemmed, or a walker, whether pick-up or wheeled type, should be determined by the needs of the individual (see the exhibit on pp. 77–78). In some ways, ambulation devices should be treated as medications: They should be "pre-

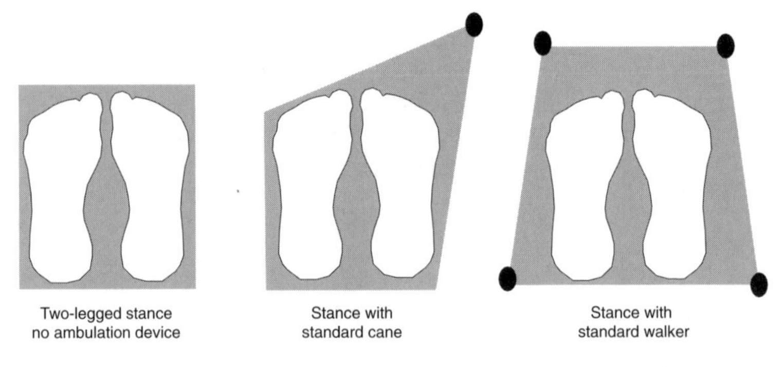

Figure 4-6. Base of support (shaded areas) provided by ambulation devices.

scribed" to correct a specific underlying gait and balance problem and, as a consequence, tailored to fit both the person and the environment. Also, individuals must be instructed in the proper use of the device in walking and transferring in order to prevent adverse effects, such as falls and subsequent injury, which is best accomplished by referring patients and residents to a physiatrist or physical therapist.

Despite best efforts to prescribe the correct device and instruct individuals in using an assistive device properly, many patients and residents use ill-fitting devices and/or use them inappropriately, which heightens the risk of falls. Nurses and other hospital and facility staff are in a position to detect errors at an early stage and to decrease fall risk through corrective intervention. Corrective intervention can be accomplished by, first, ensuring that canes and walkers are the appropriate size (Appendix B), and, second, ensuring that patients and residents are using their devices properly during activities (Appendix C). In addition to checking for the proper size or fit and correct use of devices, ambulation devices should be inspected routinely for defects (see the exhibit on p. 79). Inspection is of particular importance in nursing facilities, where the mobility status and device requirements of residents are likely to change over time.

Wheelchairs

Wheelchairs are designed for patients and residents with limited ability to walk or who are totally dependent in walking. Wheelchairs come in a variety of sizes, designs, and materials, all of which are determined

Assistive Ambulation Devices

Standard Cane

The standard cane is the most commonly used ambulation device. It is shaped like a candy cane and is usually made of wood or adjustable aluminum. The crook handle of the standard cane decreases grip strength, particularly in individuals with arthritis. The point of support is in the front of the hand, which makes this cane slightly unsteady. The cane should be held in the hand opposite to the disability (e.g., if pain is in right knee, cane is held in left hand). For balance support, however, the cane may be held in either hand.

Ortho Cane

The ortho cane is made of aluminum and is adjustable. It is similar to the standard cane. The shaft of the cane is offset, thereby placing the point of support directly below the handle. This design offers more stability than does the standard cane. The handle is molded, which provides a more comfortable grip than the standard cane.

Quad Cane

The quad cane has four legs and is used by individuals with impairment or weakness in one leg but who possess adequate balance control. This cane is more stable than the standard cane. It comes in a variety of base sizes. Base size is important because the wider the base, the greater the stability. Individuals with dementia may experience difficulty with quad canes. If the handle is not held facing the proper direction, the cane becomes very unstable, leading to loss of balance. Also, people with impaired vision may easily trip over the legs of the cane.

Hemiwalker

The hemiwalker is a one-arm walker with four legs. This walker offers more support than the quad cane due to its broadly based legs. It is designed for individuals who are unable to use a standard walker (e.g., a hemiplegic with only one functioning upper extremity). Use of the hemiwalker requires good balance control and upper arm strength to move the walker.

(continued)

Assistive Ambulation Devices (continued)

Standard Walker

The standard walker consists of four adjustable legs equipped with rubber tips. The walker is designed for individuals with poor balance and lower-extremity weakness or impairment. Walkers may be either nonfolding or folding. Nonfolding walkers offer greater stability and may be more appropriate than folding walkers for people living in long-term care facilities.

The device itself has several limitations: The individual using the walker must pick up the walker while walking, which results in a loss of balance when all four legs of the walker are off the floor. Individuals with poor balance and/or upper-extremity weakness may push the device along the floor, causing the walker to suddenly halt and tip over, a particular problem on carpeted floor coverings. Applying metal furniture tips to the legs can overcome this problem, although the walker may slide away from some individuals.

Rolling Walker

The rolling walker is similar in design to the standard walker, however, it is equipped with either two front wheels or wheels attached to all four legs. The rolling walker does not require lifting and, therefore, is suited for individuals with poor balance and limited upper-extremity strength. The two-wheeled walker is difficult to move on carpeted floor coverings because the rear legs drag along the floor; applying metal furniture tips to the rear legs overcomes this problem. The four-wheel walker is easier to move along, but may roll too far forward, causing users to lose their balance.

Rolling walkers equipped with weight-activated brakes are safer to use; the walker automatically stops when the user pushes down on the rear legs of the device. Some four-wheel walkers are equipped with baskets and seats, which allow individuals to carry objects and sit down when tired, although sitting down requires good transfer technique and sitting balance.

Ambulation Device Inspection Summary

Inspect	Examine canes and walkers for defects (e.g., worn rubber tips, defective wheels, structural problems). Replace device as indicated and/or refer all problems to Physical Therapy.
Inquire	Ask patients and residents about their device: Are they using their cane or walker? If not, why? Are they experiencing any problems with their cane or walker? If yes, what are the problems? Does the device improve or interfere with ambulation? Refer all problems to Physical Therapy.
Observe	Ask patients and residents to perform walking and transferring maneuvers with their device. Observe whether they are performing tasks correctly and safely. Are they able to use their device properly in tight places (e.g., bathroom, bedroom) without interference? Refer all problems to Physical Therapy.

by the needs of the patient or resident. It is essential for nursing and other staff to work with physical and occupational therapists to ensure proper chair selection, fit, and use. The problems most commonly causing wheelchair falls and suggestions on how to correct them are described in the checklist on page 80.

Environmental Strategies

When older people enter a hospital or nursing facility, they are exposed to new environmental conditions such as the design of furnishings, illumination, and ground surfaces. If these conditions exceed their mobility capacity, they are at risk for falls. Patients and residents with functional disabilities are especially vulnerable. These individuals have a narrower adaptive range available to them to cope with the increased demands of the environment (e.g., elevated bed heights, diminished lighting, glare-producing floor surfaces). In this context the goal of environmental interventions to reduce fall risk is twofold: 1) to identify and subsequently eliminate conditions that may interfere with mobility, and 2) to simplify or maximize individual mobility tasks by modifying the physical environment and the surrounding areas (see Chapter 5).

Wheelchair Problems and Modifications

Observe patients' or residents' wheelchair mobility. Ask each individual to transfer from the chair and observe whether he or she accomplishes the task safely.

Did the person engage the brakes? *If no, consider wedge cushion to prevent independent transfers.*	Yes	No
Can the person reach the hand brakes? *If no, replace with long brake handles.*	Yes	No
Did the brakes lock in place? *If no, replace the chair or fix the problem.*	Yes	No
Did the person remember to move the footrests away? *If no, consider removing footrests (if appropriate) or consider adding a wedge cushion to prevent independent transfers.*	Yes	No
Did the chair tip over forward? *If yes, consider attaching antitip device to footplates or weights to the back of the chair.*	Yes	No
Does the seat interfere with transfers? *If yes, consider retrofitting sling seat with plywood or solid inserts.*	Yes	No
Does the seat interfere with sitting balance? *If yes, consider lateral supports to correct lean.*	Yes	No
Does the individual slide out of chair seat? *If yes, consider use of Dycem (placed on seat to prevent sliding) or position footrests to maintain proper seating.*	Yes	No

The most important environmental items to be assessed follow. To ensure that safe conditions are maintained, a complete and comprehensive assessment should be executed on a regular basis.

Illumination

- Are lights bright enough to compensate for reduced vision?
- Are lights glare-free?
- Are light switch plates, lamp pull cords, and switches in the bedroom and bathroom both visually and physically accessible?
- Are light switches available by the entryway of bedrooms and bathrooms (to avoid ambulating in the dark)?
- Are night-lights available in the bedroom and bathroom?

Floor surfaces

- Are floor surfaces slip-resistant?
- Are carpeted edges tacked or taped down?
- Are throw rugs slip-resistant?
- Are frequently traveled pathways in the bedroom and ward area free of low-lying (i.e., difficult to visualize) objects?

Furnishings

- Are beds low in height and stable enough to support safe, independent transfers?
- Are chairs equipped with armrests, and are they stable enough (i.e., nontippable) to support safe, independent transfers?
- Are bedside and dining room tables stable enough to support balance when leaned on?

Bathroom

- Are toilet grab bars available and securely fastened to the toilet or mounted on the wall?

Fall Prevention Programs

Fall prevention programs have been developed by several hospitals and nursing facilities. These programs have met with varying degrees of success in fall reduction and have the following in common:

- A multidisciplinary safety committee to develop and implement an institution-wide fall prevention program. The members of the committee are knowledgeable about falls, conversant with the literature, and include one or more individuals (e.g., director of nursing, medical director or chief of medicine, director of quality assurance, administrator) who have the administrative authority within the institution to enact or facilitate policy change.

- An in-service nursing and medical staff education program for all professionals involved in patient and resident care on the causes of falls, factors responsible for fall risk, and appropriate preventive strategies. Nursing education extends to staff on all three shifts.
- A mechanism to identify patients and residents at fall risk immediately on admission that is available for each nursing shift. Fall risk is reassessed whenever an individual's medical condition, medication regimen, or mobility status changes.
- Identification tags (e.g., colored wrist identification bands, colored adhesive stickers near the bedroom door and bedside and on medical/nursing charts)—ID tags are used to alert staff to people at great risk for falls.
- Assessment of patients and residents immediately after a fall. Patients and residents are evaluated for underlying medical and environmental causes. A formal program and policy for reporting and investigating incident reports is in place. The essential components of both are described on pages 83 and 84.
- Strategies are implemented to prevent falls, and follow-up to review whether the designed interventions have decreased falls occurs on a regular basis. These preventive strategies are presented on page 85. (This list is not meant to be all-inclusive, nor does it suggest that these strategies are effective. It represents those recommendations most commonly found in the literature.)
- An educational program for patients, residents, and family members, which teaches the causes and prevention of falls during a stay in the hospital or nursing facility (see p. 86).
- A discharge teaching program for patients, residents, and family members, which teaches the prevention of risks of readmission (see p. 87).

Components of Policy for Incident Reporting

The policy clearly defines what events constitute a reportable fall (e.g., an unanticipated event, usually of sudden onset, in which the patient or resident engages in an activity that results in balance loss and a subsequent fall).

The policy clearly describes what actions to take in the event of injury and/or acute medical conditions.

The policy clearly describes fall precaution measures to follow in order to prevent recurrence.

The policy clearly outlines a step-by-step procedure to follow for completing the incident report.

The policy clearly describes a step-by-step process to follow after the incident report is completed (e.g., documenting the incident in the patient's or resident's chart, forwarding a copy of the incident report for administrative review to the medical and nursing director, safety committee, or quality assurance committee).

The policy describes a process to inform all staff involved in patient or resident care of the current policy (e.g., during orientation, during in-service education).

The policy describes a time period in which statements are updated to reflect institutional attempts to practice reasonable standards of care related to fall prevention.

Components of Incident Report

- ✍ Time and place of the fall.
- ✍ Injuries and/or medical conditions present at the time and results of the medical examination.
- ✍ Circumstance of the fall (patient/resident description of the event and/or eyewitness reports).
- ✍ Fall risk factors, both intrinsic and extrinsic, present at the time of the fall. Was the patient or resident at risk?
- ✍ Preventive measures in place at the time of the fall, especially if the individual was at risk.
- ✍ Immediate preventive strategies put in place to prevent additional falls.
- ✍ Recommendations for treatment (i.e., intervention strategies) to prevent fall recurrence.

- The consistent recognition of staff (i.e., given a "pat on the back"). They are informed that their efforts have led to a reduction of falls and an enhanced level of care. Praise has been conveyed through announcements in newsletters or special plaques presented by the administration.

Although further research is needed, there is ample evidence to suggest that incorporating these components into existing or newly developed fall prevention programs is beneficial in reducing fall risk.

Strategies for Fall Prevention

Assessment

Identify fall risk on admission.

After admission, reassess risk level at regular intervals (e.g., daily, every shift, changes in medical and/or functional conditions).

Observe patient or resident mobility on a daily basis.

Monitor high-risk medications (side effects), polypharmacy.

Conduct environmental safety rounds on a regular basis (e.g., check wheelchair brakes/footrests, bed wheel brakes, bed side rail attachments, nonslip strips along the side of the bed, safety of assistive ambulation devices, condition of floor coverings, position of furnishings in bedroom, safety of bedside commodes, clutter in hallways, night-lights in bedroom, safety of footwear).

Nursing Care

Maintain regular toileting schedules (elimination rounds).

Use bedside commodes during hours of sleep.

Provide properly fitting, nonslip footwear.

Place confused patients or residents close to nurses' station for close observation.

Establish frequent nursing rounds on high-risk patients or residents.

Provide assistive ambulation.

Encourage daily exercise.

Increase nursing staff.

Environmental

Keep bed in a low position.

Keep the bed wheels locked.

Use bed half side rails to assist with safe bed transfers.

Place the call light and other objects within easy patient or resident reach.

Use bed/chair alarm systems to monitor unsafe activity.

Maintain adequate illumination in bedrooms and bathrooms.

Maintain nonslip floor surfaces.

Keep hallways clear.

Provide grab bars and toilet risers in the bathroom.

Educational Program for Patients, Residents, and Family Members

To reduce the risk of falls during a stay in the hospital or nursing facility:

Orient patients or residents to bedroom, unit, activities, and routines.

Orient patients or residents to staff members.

Instruct patients or residents on the proper use of equipment (e.g., electric beds, call lights, ambulation devices, wheelchairs, bathroom grab bars, bed half side rails, bedside commodes). Do not assume that individuals can figure out these things by themselves.

Teach patients or residents safe transfer techniques from bed, chairs, toilet, and wheelchair.

Instruct high-risk patients or residents to call for assistance when getting out of bed, ambulating, and toileting.

Educate family members about safety measures and fall prevention; provide instruction on how to identify risk and environmental hazards.

Provide a safety brochure that addresses important issues such as the need to wear nonslip footwear and use assistive devices whenever out of bed, the importance of calling for assistance during periods of increased risk, important side effects of medications, what to do if a fall occurs, and so forth. Material should be printed in large type for easier reading and reinforced verbally with patients or residents and family members at the time of admission.

Discharge Teaching Program

To reduce the risk of falls and related injury at home:

Prevent the risk of down time (i.e., person is unable to arise unassisted from the floor following a fall). Provide patient or resident with a personal emergency response system (PERS). This is a button device worn by the individual as a pendant or wrist band and a radio transmitter connected to the person's home telephone. When the device is activated, the emergency signal goes out to a 24-hour monitoring center, which sends appropriate help (e.g., family member, neighbor, police, ambulance). The PERS can be purchased, leased, or rented. As an alternative, individuals can be taught how to rise from the floor by themselves (i.e., move themselves to a side-sitting position). They can then kneel with the support of a chair and, using the strongest knee, push themselves up into the chair.

Teach home safety. Provide the patient or resident with information about how to prevent falls in the home. In addition, patients or residents with mobility impairment should receive a home safety evaluation from physical or occupational therapists and instruction on home medical equipment required (e.g., walkers, wheelchairs, toilet and bathtub devices). Remember that equipment used in the hospital or nursing facility may not be adequate to support safe mobility in the home.

Notes

[1]Shields sewn into specially designed undergarments: SAFEHIP, Sahvatex, Phone: +45-9725-0855 (Denmark). Foam pads sewn into specially designed undergarments: HIPSAVERS, The HipSaver Company, Inc., 7 Hubbard Street, Canton, Massachusetts USA 02021. Phone: 1-800-358-HIPS. Shields placed into pockets of ordinary undergarments: HIPS, Simonsen and Weel, Erik Husfeldtsvej 2, DK-2630 Tastrup (Denmark). Phone: +45-4355-5500. Foam pads inserted into wraparound garment: HIP-GUARD, Prevent-Wise, Inc., Post Office Box 909, Jackson Heights, New York USA 11372. Phone: 718-899-5734. Adhesive pads applied to skin: NEOFLEX, Roland Healthcare, Hvidehusvej 34, DK-3450 Allerod (Denmark). Phone: +45-4814-2080.

[2]Lauritzen, J.B., Peterson, M.M., & Lund, B. (1993). Effect of external hip protectors on hip fractures. *Lancet*, 341, 11–13.

[3]Ekman, A., Mallmin, H., Michaelsson, K., & Ljunghall, S. (1997). External hip protectors to prevent osteoporotic hip fractures. *Lancet*, 350, 563–564.

chapter five

Environmental Modifications

Older adults residing in hospitals and nursing facilities differ in their functional capacity: Some have no limitations, whereas others experience partial to severe loss of function. For people with diminished physical capacity, the physical environment takes on greater significance. It either can contribute to hazardous mobility and increase the risk of falls or it can be utilized as a resource to compensate for individual mobility problems and reduce the risk of falls. For example, poor lighting increases the degree of functional visual loss and adversely affects ambulation, but it can be improved to provide a level of illumination that facilitates safe walking. Low-seated chairs without armrests can cause unsafe transfers in people with diminished muscular strength. Furniture can be made more supportive with the addition of seat cushions and armrests.

Environmental modification can serve as a powerful adaptive strategy for patients and residents with decreased mobility to promote mobility and reduce the likelihood of falling. Thus, the design of institutional environments and any subsequent adjustments must transcend appearances and be based on activity-based standards: Function must take precedence over aesthetics. Put plainly, in structure and design, floor surfaces and coverings, lighting, and furnishings should 1) maximize or support ambulation and transferring function and 2) be aesthetically pleasing. This chapter focuses on aspects of the hospital and nursing facility environment that are most likely to contribute to unsafe mobility and that suggest corrective modification.

Lighting

The aspect of lighting itself is influenced by numerous factors, including illumination, location, quality, changes in intensity, access, and glare reduction.

Illumination

The proper amount of illumination in the environment is dependent on the visual needs of patients and residents. As a rule of thumb, older people require two to three times more light than do younger people to facilitate vision because of the aging-related decline in visual functioning. This is, however, a generalization. In some cases, lower levels of lighting may be more appropriate than higher levels. For instance, people with cataracts or glaucoma tend to be sensitive to bright light. For these individuals, any increase in lighting may impair their vision and increase their fall risk.

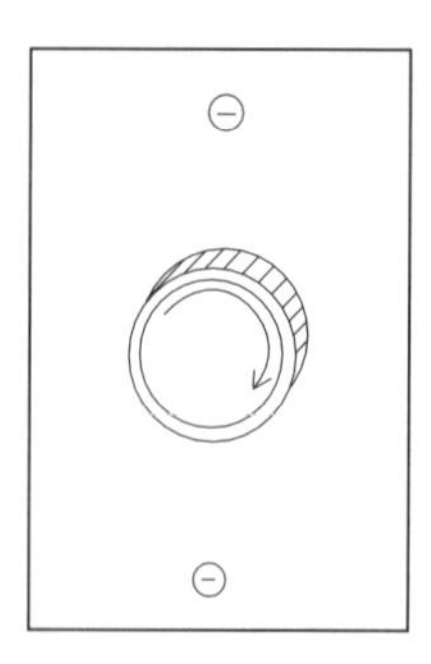

Figure 5-1. Rheostatic light switch.

Under ideal circumstances, the control of lighting levels should rest with the individual so that he or she is able to regulate and maintain a level of illumination that is both visually comfortable and safe for mobility. Rheostatic light switches allow a person to increase or decrease illumination levels as desired (Figure 5-1). However, patient or resident control of lighting may not always be possible, especially with individuals who are cognitively impaired or in wheelchairs. The best way to help determine the lighting needs of an individual is to observe the person in his or her environment and note any difficulties encountered. Correction may call for an increase, a decrease, or a redistribution in lighting levels.

Strategic Lighting

Extra lighting may be needed in certain locations, such as the bedroom, because they represent a high fall risk. The path from the bedside to the bathroom may be difficult to visualize, especially at night when patients and residents may get up to go to the bathroom. In an attempt to provide adequate illumination and safe passage, staff members sometimes leave the bathroom light on throughout the night. The bright bathroom light, however, may interfere with sleep or may temporarily blind the person with a sudden flooding of bright light when he or she enters the bathroom. Conversely, leaving a bright bathroom and walking into a dark bedroom can cause similar problems because older eyes readjust to lighting levels more slowly than do younger eyes.

A bedside lamp with a secure base that will not tip over, a light attached to the headboard within easy reach, or a night-light can be used to provide adequate illumination and facilitate safe ambulation (Figure 5-2). A light can be installed under the apron of a bedside table or nightstand to provide night lighting, or night-lights can be positioned close to the floor along the path leading from the bedroom to the bathroom. Motion-sensor lighting located in the bathroom is also a good solution.

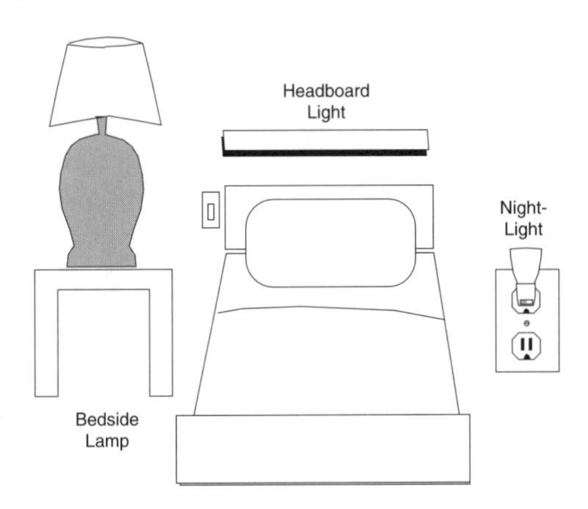

Figure 5-2. Lighting sources that increase illumination.

Effective Lighting Sources

In addition to an adequate quantity of illumination, the quality of available lighting is important for safe ambulation. Full-spectrum fluorescent lighting is much more effective than incandescent lighting for overall illumination in the environment. Blue fluorescent light simulates natural sunlight, providing light that is spread evenly, continuous, and free of shadows. However, the best effects are produced by a bulb emitting light that is in the yellow spectrum. Halogen lamps produce light that is more like natural sunlight and freer from glare than either fluorescent or incandescent fixtures. Halogen lamps are particularly effective for task lighting, illuminating specific areas in the bedroom and bathroom.

Lighting Changes

The ability of the eye to adapt to changes in illumination decreases with age. Any sudden change in light intensity—that which occurs when a person moves from a dark to a bright area and vice versa—should be avoided because it can lead to momentary visual loss and increase the risk of falls. Perhaps the most common example involves patients and residents traveling at night from a darkened bedroom into the bathroom and turning on the light. Rheostatic light switches that vary the amount of available light can ensure an even distribution of light and prevent such sudden and pronounced shifts in illumination that may occur with toggle light switches. Another alternative is to use compact fluorescent bulbs in transition areas or in rooms and areas where older people encounter dramatic changes in light levels. These bulbs take approximately 1 minute to heat to full brightness, minimizing the adjustment from darkness to light. Night-lights can be used in the bedroom and bathroom as well, but are not as effective. Also, night-lights can produce frightening shadows or create an illusion of steps or edges where light and shadows meet.

Lighting Access

All environmental lighting should be physically accessible to patients and residents. Light switches should be positioned approximately 32 inches off the floor and located directly on the outside or inside of doorways to help people avoid walking across a darkened room to turn on a light (Figure 5-3). The color of the switch plates should contrast that of the wall to allow for improved visibility. If the wall and switch plate colors are identical, the switch plate should be painted in a contrasting color or adhesive tape in a contrasting color can be placed around the borders of the switch plate to enhance its visibility. A small light located within the switch or an illuminated switch plate will allow for improved visibility and access at night. Pressure-plate controls are easier to use than standard toggle switches. The pull cord that controls bedside lighting should be long enough for users to avoid excessive reaching and risk loss of balance. In addition, the pull cord should be in a contrasting color so that it can be seen easily by the older user.

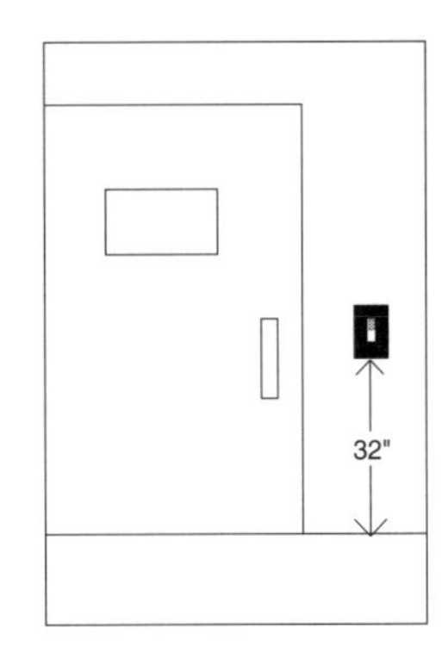

Figure 5-3. For ease in reaching, the light switch should be located 32 inches in height from the floor.

Glare Reduction

Glare from sunlight shining through windows, skylights, or other light sources such as fluorescent lights reflecting directly on polished waxed floors, on furnishings such as laminated tabletops, and on plastic chair seats produces discomfort or disability glare and can impair a person's vision. Draperies or adjustable venetian blinds can be used to block sunlight from windows. Unfortunately, they reduce the amount of available light and may not present the best solution to glare. Furthermore, horizontal and vertical blinds, with their tilting capability, cause sunlight to be deflected, creating light patterns on the floor that can be confusing visually. Polarized window glass or tinted Mylar shades eliminate glare without loss of ambient light. Another solution is to use translucent light-filtering pleated shades or sheer draperies, which diffuse light and offer some degree of light and glare regulation.

Floor glare can be controlled by using carpeting or nongloss floor waxes and finishes that diffuse rather than reflect light and eliminate glare. Also, wall-mounted valances or cove lighting that conceal the source of light and spread it indirectly on the ceiling and floor serve the same purpose. Matte or dull finishes on tabletops and nonreflective material on chair seats can help prevent surface glare.

Floor Surfaces

Floor surfaces can be dangerous for individuals with gait and balance impairments. By identifying dangerous flooring conditions and applying some simple modifications to make floor surfaces safer, the risk of falls and injury can be reduced greatly.

Ceramic and Linoleum Surfaces

Highly polished or wet flooring can contribute to slip-related falls. In addition, highly buffed and polished flooring can cause reflected glare, the result of lighting sources shining directly on it. Glare can give floors the appearance of being wet or slick, creating a source fear of falling and/or injury in some older people and leading to uncertainty or a reluctance on the part of the patient or resident to walk on the floor surface. Floor surfaces that inhibit ambulation can be viewed as a form of passive restraint, a condition resulting in mobility restrictions.

Two modifications are helpful in eliminating these hazards: First, ceramic tiles and linoleum floors must be slip-resistant, particularly when wet. Unglazed tiles, which are nonslip by design, can be used in the bathroom, or slip-resistant adhesive strips can be applied to the floor next to the sink and toilet, locations that are prone to water and urine spillage (Figure 5-4). The color of the adhesive strips should match that of the floor surface to prevent easy visualization. Older people, especially those with altered depth perception or dementia, may misinterpret color-contrasted floor strips, perceiving them as ground elevations or depressions and, as a result, they attempt to avoid them. They may try to step over the strips, thereby actually increasing their risk of falls because of alterations in gait and balance. Because the purpose of adhesive strips is to help render the floor slip-resistant, it

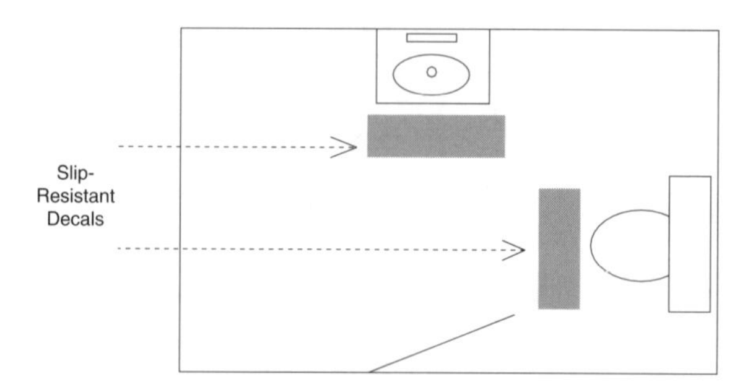

Figure 5-4. Slip-resistant adhesive strips are applied to the floor by the sink and toilet.

is not necessary for them to be seen. Sheet rubber flooring in the bathroom can be used as an alternate method of slip resistance.

The second modification is to make linoleum floors slip-resistant by applying antiskid acrylic coatings or by using no-wax sheet vinyl flooring. If tile and vinyl flooring are waxed, minimal buffing after waxing helps to reduce slipping and eliminates glare. Using nongloss wax, as opposed to high-gloss finishes, on flooring also corrects glare.

All flooring should be flush and even to prevent patients and residents from tripping on it. Doorway thresholds, such as those on the floor between the bedroom and bathroom, should be avoided or eliminated. Thresholds create a problem for older people who have poor eyesight and/or difficulty lifting their feet to clear obstacles.

Carpeting

Carpeting offers several advantages in hospital and nursing facility settings: It provides a slip-resistant surface and cushion that helps to reduce the risk of injury following a fall. In particular, indoor-outdoor carpeting in the bathroom is beneficial in that it traps water or other liquids, such as urine, that may be present, and dries quickly, thereby reducing the likelihood of slipping. As compared with vinyl flooring, a carpeted bedroom floor greatly reduces the risk of injury from a fall by providing a much softer surface on which to land.[1] Carpeting also has acoustic value in that it reduces echo resulting from shoes striking tile and linoleum flooring.

Carpeting has disadvantages as well. Older adults who use wheeled walkers and wheelchairs may experience difficulty rolling these assistive devices over carpeted surfaces, especially those that are thick. Patients and residents who push along pick-up–style walkers rather than lift up and put down the walker with each step also may experience problems with carpeting. The legs of the walker can catch on the carpet, causing an older person to lose his or her balance and fall. In addition, individuals who walk with a shuffling gait may find that thick carpeting impedes safe mobility and increases the risk of tripping.

Despite concerns about carpeting, institutions should not be discouraged from using it because, when properly chosen, their advantages far outweigh any disadvantages. Uncut low-pile carpeting is the best choice for institutional settings because this surface is least likely to interfere with walking and using walkers and wheelchairs. Deep-pile carpeting should be avoided. Aside from interfering with safe ambulation, dense carpets can cause a loss of proprioceptive feedback and balance, which are gained from the feet striking the ground. Carpet tiles are usually not recommended in institutional settings, as the number of seams between the tiles creates an opportunity for liquids to seep into the underlayer. The greatest concern is that of urine, the odor of which becomes offensive to patients or residents, staff, and visitors alike.

Carpets made of nylon fibers provide a smooth walking surface and possess excellent strength and durability, beneficial features in areas subject to heavy traffic and soiling. The color of the carpeting should contrast that of the walls to help older people, especially individuals with impaired depth perception, define the boundary between the floor and wall. A person's balance may be affected adversely when this distinction is not made clear. Patterns such as floral or checkered configurations, although pleasing to look at, should be avoided because they can lead to misjudgment of spatial distances. Misperception is heightened in people with a visual dysfunction, such as cataracts and poor depth perception, and dementia (i.e., patterns seem to move, leading to increased confusion and feeling unbalanced). Plain, unpatterned carpeting is less confusing both visually and intellectually. All carpeting should be checked periodically for curled edges and excessive wear in order to guard against tripping.

Transitions from one type of floor surface to another must be as smooth and level as possible (i.e., no higher than ¼ inch) to accommodate wheelchairs, shuffling feet, and ambulation assistive devices. Changes in floor surfaces should be avoided in areas prone to shifts in lighting because the eyes of older adults need time to adjust to changing light levels, and these individuals may not recognize changes in surfaces in time to adjust their gait. Transitions in floor surfaces should occur only in locations where lighting is sufficient and constant.

Hallways

Hallways can present an obstacle for patients and residents. Long hallways are a particular problem because they require older people with mobility problems to travel a considerable distance to reach the nurses' station, dining rooms, and so forth. As a result, patients and residents may be reluctant to walk distances, especially if they become fatigued easily, experience balance problems, or fear falling. One solution to this problem is to move the patient or resident to a bedroom that is located closer to the nurses' station and other commonly used areas. However, relocation may not be easy to achieve or safe; for example, new environments may be disorienting for people with dementia. A more realistic and perhaps better solution is to provide "rest stops," or chairs strategically placed every 20–30 feet, along long hallways. These rest stops allow older individuals to rest whenever they become tired or unsteady and to continue their journey when they feel better.

Hallways and traffic lanes can become cluttered with medicine, laundry and food carts, cleaning equipment, wheelchairs, unused walkers, and poorly placed furniture, presenting an obstacle and interfering with safe ambulation. Clutter should be avoided as much as possible. Because many older people lose peripheral vision, they can easily bump into objects located in their path and may trip or lose balance as a result. Moreover, cluttered hallways can obstruct a person's view of handrails or access to them.

Handrail Support

In all areas used by ambulating patients and residents, handrails should be installed to provide support (e.g., enhance balance, encourage movement, allay fear of falling). Handrails are especially helpful in areas with poor footing (e.g., polished or slick flooring) and abrasive wall finishes or coverings, which can cut into fragile aging skin easily if walls are relied on for mobility support (i.e., hand or shoulder support) and brushed up against. Handrails are most effective for gripping if they are round in shape rather than flat. Round handrails allow a person's thumb and forefingers to meet; flat handrails are difficult to grasp, particularly for people with arthritic hands, and are less effective than round handrails for maintaining support. In addition, the color of the handrails should contrast that of the walls to promote easy visibility, should be nonslip (e.g., a wraparound cover of textured vinyl) when grasped, and should be located approximately 2 inches from the wall and 26–36 inches above the floor for easy access (Figure 5-5). Handrails that are well designed and well placed allow older people to grasp the rails and glide along them. They also allow individuals to lean on their forearms for added support.

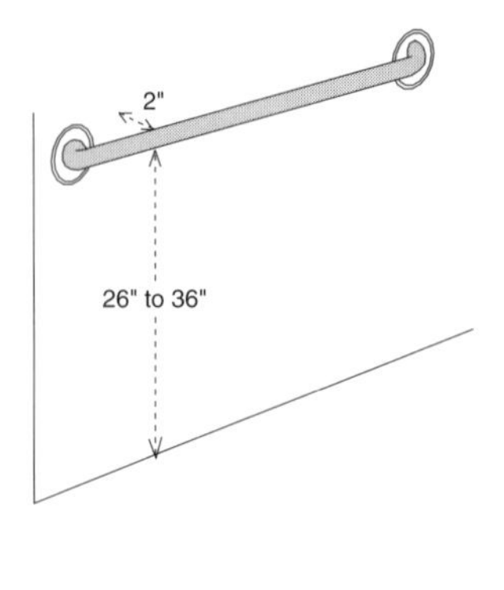

Figure 5-5. Handrail support should be located 26–36 inches in height from the floor.

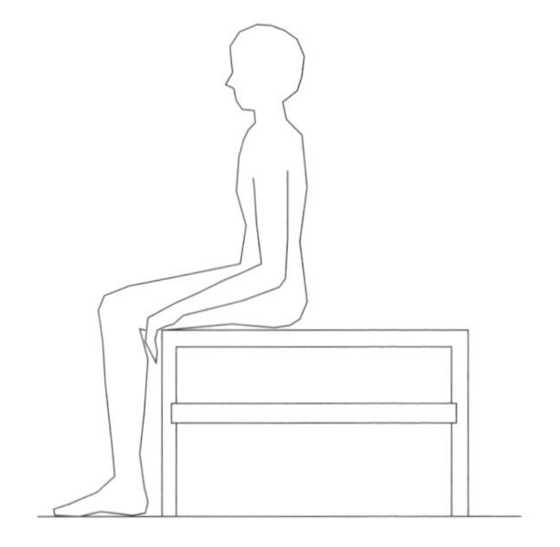

Figure 5-6. Bed height is appropriate when the person is able to sit with the knees flexed at 90° and both feet planted firmly on the floor.

Beds

For patients and residents with diminished bed-mobility skills, modification of the bed and its surrounding area can support safe mobility.

Bed Height

Bed height is defined as the distance from the floor to the top of the mattress. Bed height is appropriate when a person is able to sit on the edge of the mattress with the knees flexed at 90° and plant both feet firmly on the floor (Figure 5-6). A bed height that is safe enough to support transfer activity can be obtained with the use of height-adjustable "hi-low" beds. Because the "hi-low" bed can be lowered to any level desired, it can provide a greater sense of security and confidence to patients and residents, which promotes independence and ease of transfers. If the height of the bed is still too great despite the use of this mechanism, a thinner mattress may be used to achieve the desired height. Because bed height may be altered routinely in order to change linens or perform routine nursing care, staff should check the height periodically to ensure that it is maintained at a level that is appropriate for the patient or resident. Also, if the beds are controlled manually with crank handles, staff should check that the handles are recessed underneath the bed at all times so that they do not constitute a tripping hazard.

Institutional bed design has changed dramatically since 1995. Most likely, this change occurred in response to the persistent problem that falls from bed represent for hospitals and nursing facilities and to a general dissatisfaction with the type of beds available. As a result, the variety of beds on the market fit an assortment of needs.[2] Apart from a new generation of "hi-low" beds, which can be positioned at varying heights ranging from near-floor level to elevations considerably higher than standard beds, several models of fixed low-deck height beds are available. These beds have a mattress deck height of 5½–7 inches above the level of the floor and are designed to eliminate the use of mechanical restraints in patients and residents at risk for falling from bed. The use of the "hi-low" bed can replace the common practice of placing the older person's mattress or double mattress directly on the floor to eliminate falls from bed. Although placing the mattress on the floor is effective, family members can become upset over seeing their loved one lying on the mattress, especially if the floor or carpet is not clean. In this case, families may find fixed low-height beds a better alternative. In addition, these beds are equipped with casters, which permit the bed to be moved when the floor is cleaned.

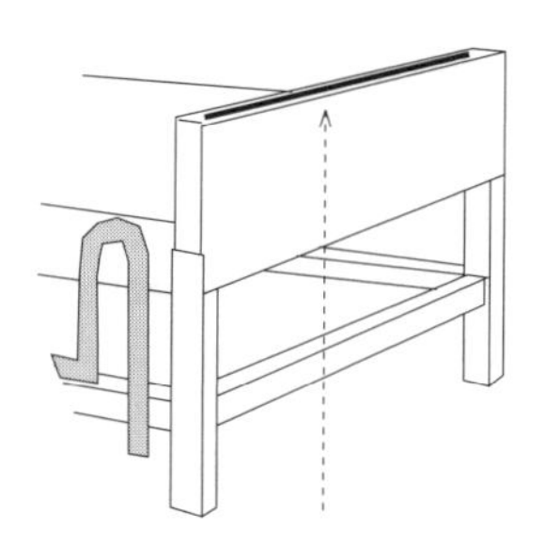

Figure 5-7. Nonslip adhesive strip is placed along the footboard to support mobility.

Bed Supports

Sometimes patients and residents with poor bed or walking mobility may use the footboard as an aid in transferring in and out of bed or in ambulating about the bedroom. To provide adequate support, the footboard should be easy to grasp and slip-resistant (Figure 5-7). Nonslip adhesive strips placed along the top length of the footboard prevent hands from slipping. A color-contrasted strip on the footboard can help a person to recognize it more easily, calls attention to the board itself, and helps prevent the person from bumping into the bed.

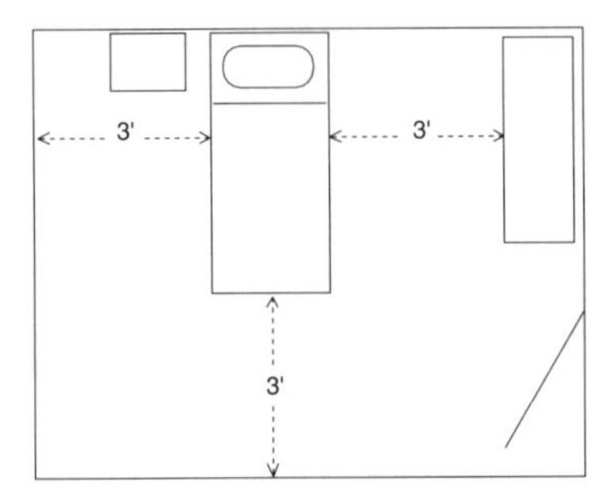

Figure 5-8. Bedroom circulation space for safe ambulation.

In addition, an adequate amount of space between the bed and other furnishings should be created to allow for safe ambulation and transferring, particularly if walkers are used. A circulation space of at least 3 feet wide provides enough room for patient or resident movement with or without ambulation devices (Figure 5-8).

Mattresses

Patients and residents with poor sitting balance may be at risk for falling from bed if mattress edges sag or slouch. An overly soft mattress does not provide the support necessary for safe bed transfers, particularly if these individuals rely on hand support to accomplish them. All mattresses should be firm enough to support older adults securely when they are seated in an upright position. Mattress edges that are rolled offer them a good grasping surface when transferring (Figure 5-9).

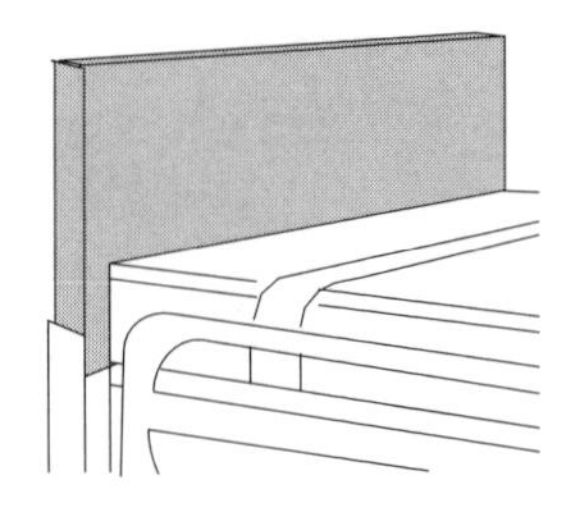

Figure 5-9. Rolled mattress edge.

Bed Side Rails

Bed side rails have both disadvantages and advantages. As mentioned previously, bed side rails in the raised position can contribute to falls and physical injury. For example, patients and residents who are agile may climb over the top of the rail and become entangled in it. If they are used properly, bed side rails offer real benefits, providing safety and assistance in bed transfers. When positioned at least 14 inches above the top of the mattress full-length bed side rails can help prevent people under sedation from rolling and falling out of bed unexpectedly. With one full-length bed side rail up on the opposite side of the bed, patients and residents are reminded of the side of the bed from which they should exit. However, full-length rails should not be used for individuals who are able to get out of bed. A better choice is to use half bed side rails, which do not interfere with exiting but help prevent older adults from rolling out of bed inadvertently.

Many patients and residents are accustomed to sleeping on a wider bed surface at home, and in the hospital or nursing facility they must adjust to sleeping in a smaller bed. The standard hospital bed has several inches or, sometimes, several feet less space than what older adults are used to, increasing their risk for rolling out of bed. People with dementia or confusion may not be able to make the adjustment to a smaller bed surface, so they are at particular risk. Also, nurse call bell cords that are out of reach can cause rolling or falling out of bed because people may lose their balance while attempting to reach the call bell.

Placing a pillow or rolled blanket under the mattress edge to create a lip or "bumper" guard can be used to prevent individuals from rolling out of bed, but this intervention may lead to transfer problems when exiting beds. Some staff have adopted the practice of placing a mattress on the floor alongside the bed to prevent injuries if a fall from bed occurs. This strategy, however, may cause additional problems; for example, older people and even staff members may trip over the mattress if left in place when the bed is not occupied. In addition, staff may need to place and remove the mattress several times a day, which can lead to noncompliance with this strategy. A soft pad, such as the FALL-EZ Mat,[3] placed on the floor may be tried as an alternative. The FALL-EZ Mat is a 35-inch-wide, 70-inch-long, 2-inch-thick mat of durable vinyl, constructed with specially designed foam to accommodate the sudden impact of a fall. The mat can be walked on and left in place while direct care is provided.

Appropriately placed half bed side rails can function as assistive or enabling devices, supporting people, such as those with Parkinsonism or stroke, with poor sitting and transfer balance (Figure 5-10). Also, the rails can help older adults build confidence in their ability to safely transfer from bed, thus, reducing their fear of falling. When used as

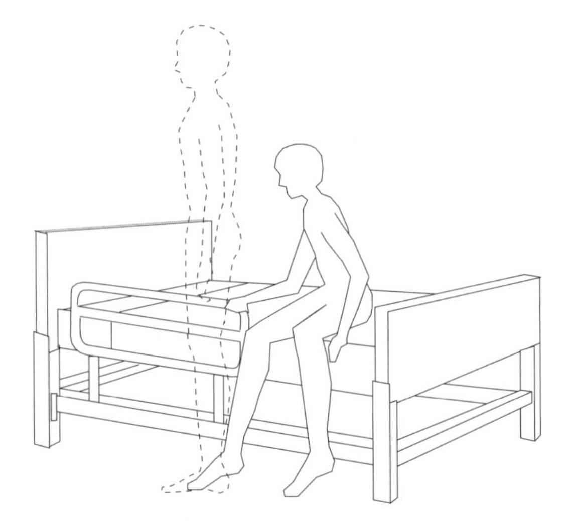

Figure 5-10. Half bed side rail used as an assistive device.

enabling devices, conventional bed side rails have some design problems. Some bed side rails are hard to grasp securely, especially for people with upper extremity dysfunction; also, bed side rails may not be secure enough to support bed transfers. As an alternative, transfer handles are available: They mount to metal bed frames, providing good stability, which allows older individuals to pull themselves up and out of bed. If bed side rails or transfer handles are used in transfers as safety devices rather than as restraints, it is a good idea to document this use in the chart. When bed side rails are not in use and are in the down position, they should recess completely underneath the bed to prevent people from climbing on the rails to enter or leave the bed.

Routine bed side rail use has long been considered standard practice in hospitals and nursing facilities. However, even half rail use should not be ordered routinely without asking a few questions: What do you hope to achieve with the use of bed side rails (e.g., will they prevent or facilitate physical and cognitive function)? Does the older person want you to use bed side rails? (Patients and residents have the right to refuse bed side rails. If patients and residents cannot make their preferences known, family members should be consulted.)

Bed Wheels

Bed wheels constitute a special hazard because they may roll or slide away during patient and resident transfers. Although all beds, including those with adequate wheel-locking systems, are unsteady to some degree, a combination swivel-and-wheel brake provides the most stability. Even when bed wheels lock properly, the bed may slide, especially if the wheels are resting on a slippery linoleum floor. To prevent sliding, the flooring can be rendered slip-resistant by placing nonslip adhesive strips or decals on the floor directly underneath the wheels (Figure 5-11). Beds that are equipped with immobilizer legs—the wheels recess when the legs are down on the floor—are acceptable alternatives to sliding bed wheels or malfunctioning locking systems (Figure 5-12).

A slippery floor surface surrounding the bed area can cause the feet of older adults to slide during bed transfers. Slippage can be prevented: Placing nonslip adhesive strips on the floor along the length of the bed provides the feet with a slip-resistant surface (Figure 5-13). The color of the nonslip strips should blend with the color of the floor so that people with altered depth perception do not misinterpret the strips as hazards. In addition, patients and residents should wear slip-resistant footwear when transferring in and out of bed. Some older people may not take the time to put on slippers when exiting bed. For these individuals, socks with nonslip or traction soles are a good choice.

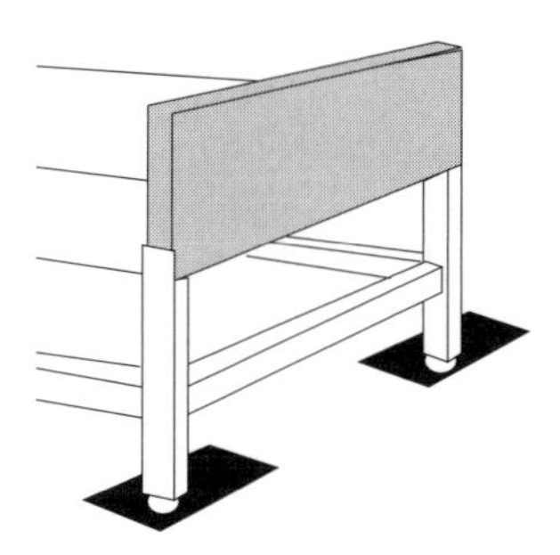

Figure 5-11. Nonslip adhesive strips placed underneath the bed wheels prevent slippage.

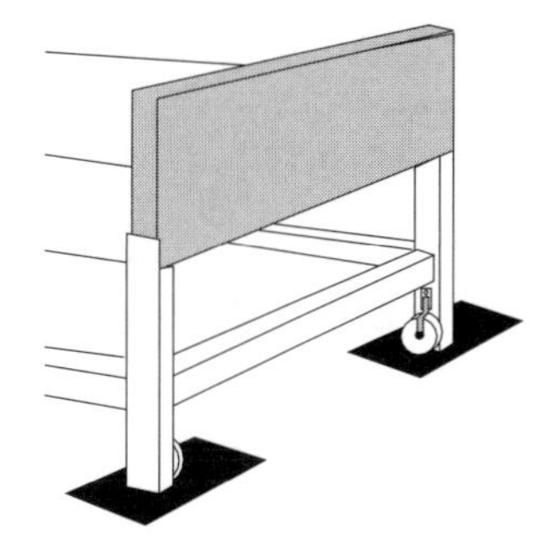

Figure 5-12. Bed with immobilizer legs.

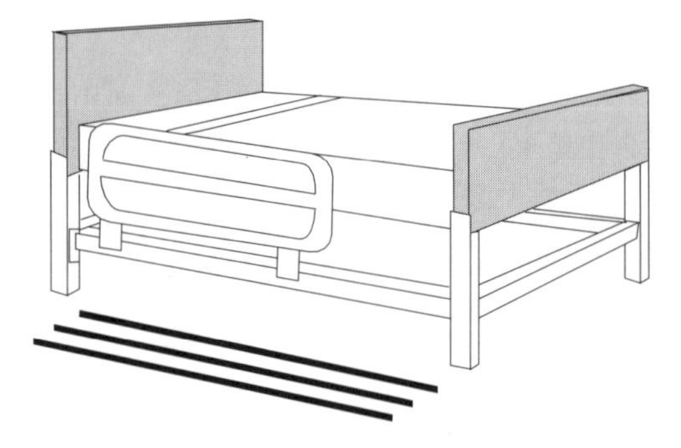

Figure 5-13. Nonslip adhesive strips are placed on the floor to prevent falls.

Bed Alarm Systems

Even after instituting comprehensive bed modifications, a certain number of patients and residents remain at risk for falls. People with cognitive dysfunction (e.g., dementia, depression, delirium) are at particular risk. Cognitive losses can cause errors in judgment, such as an inability to recognize a difference between safe and hazardous bed transfers. People with neuromuscular disorders—Parkinson's disease, stroke—and poor bed mobility who fail to ask for staff assistance are also at risk. In an effort to avoid the use of mechanical or chemical restraints, some institutions use nursing assistants or family members as in-room sitters for patients and residents at risk for bed falls. In other institutions nurses conduct hourly "bed rounds," usually at night, checking on the safety of patients and residents while in bed. Both interventions are costly because they require extra nursing staff. Bed alarm systems can be used as alternatives to in-room sitters and bed rounds and help staff avoid the use of mechanical restraints to prevent bed falls. Bed alarms are designed to warn nursing staff that patients or residents who should not attempt to leave their bed unassisted are doing so.

A variety of bed alarm systems are available, some of which attach to both the bed and the patient or resident, some to the individual alone, and others to the bed alone (see the list on p. 105). All systems function similarly and allow people to maintain a free-movement zone, or area adequate for normal bed activity. If the patient or resident leaves the bed and exceeds the free-movement zone, an alarm sounds in the bedroom, the nurses' station, or both, indicating that the indi-

Bed Alarm Systems

Bed and Patient- or Resident-Attached Systems

Bed and patient- or resident-attached alarms consist of a sensor unit mounted to the bed headboard and garment clip (cord), which attaches to the individual's night clothing. When the person attempts to leave his or her bed, the cord detaches from the sensor unit, sounding an alarm.

Posey Personal Alarm
Posey Company
Phone (800) 824-4490

Patient-Bed Exit Notifier
Dwyer Precision
Phone (800) 422-3894

Tabs Mobility Monitor
Senior Technologies, Inc.
Phone (800) 824-4490

Bed-Attached Systems

Bed-attached alarms consist of a signal unit mounted on the headboard and a pressure-sensitive sensor pad or strip placed either underneath the bed linens or mattress. When the individual attempts to leave the bed, the sensor strip detects the absence of weight and sounds the alarm. Some systems are equipped with a receiver console, which can be kept at the nurses' station.

RN+ Fall Prevention Systems
Tactilitics, Inc.
5595 Arapahoe Road, Suite B
Boulder, Colorado 80303
Phone (800) 727-1868

Bed Tender
Secure Care Products, Inc.
Phone (800) 451-7917

Bed Exit Alarm
Crest Health Care
Phone (800) 328-8908

Bed Exit Alert System
SoundMat Systems, Inc.
Phone (800) 600-8730

Bed-Check
Bed-Check Corp.
Phone (800) 523-7956

Bed Sense
Curbell
Phone (800) 235-7500

Patient- or Resident-Attached Systems

Patient- or resident-attached alarms consist of a small plastic-enclosed unit that attaches to the individual's upper leg with a fabric band. When the person attempts to leave the bed, the device shifts from the horizontal to the vertical position and sounds the alarm.

Ambularm
Alert Care, Inc.
Phone (800) 826-7444

vidual is about to transfer from the bed. All systems, according to reports, are user-friendly; safe for patients and residents in that they cause no adverse effects; and easy to install, operate, and maintain. Some institutions use homemade bed alarm devices such as baby monitors or motion detectors, which alert staff to the person stirring or leaving the bed, and nurse call light cords or personal security alarms with pull cord fastened to bed clothing, which sounds an alarm when the person exits the bed. Although these devices are less costly than commercially available systems, they may not be as effective: They sometimes fail to work by not sounding an alarm or detecting bed movement, and they break down easily.

Nurses in both hospital and nursing facility settings perceive bed alarms as capable of reducing the risk of falling and the need for mechanical restraints. Bed alarms, which do not require active participation by patients or residents to trigger, are preferable to nurse call systems, which demand active participation by individuals to activate. Institutions that use bed alarm systems as part of an overall fall prevention program have reduced bed falls by up to 85%.[4,5] Without exception, concerned family members of patients and residents prefer alarm systems to the use of restraints, citing the preservation of dignity and autonomy they offer.

The use of bed alarms should be based on a set of criteria that indicate that the patient or resident is at risk for bed falls:

- Patient or resident experiences fall(s) from bed
- Patient or resident experiences fall(s) while ambulating in bedroom or bathroom shortly after leaving bed or is found on floor after an unwitnessed fall
- Patient or resident demonstrates unsafe bed transfers
- Patient or resident has a history of cognitive/communicative problems (e.g., forgets to use call bell or ask for assistance with bed transfers)
- Patient or resident has a history of nocturia (i.e., excessive urination at night)

Once a decision has been reached to use an alarm system, individual patient and resident characteristics should determine which type is the most appropriate. A number of factors may determine choice: For example, people with dementia may become confused and agitated by the use of systems that attach to their bodies. It may be better to use pressure-sensitive systems that rest on or lie underneath the mattress and out of view. Pressure-sensitive systems that have a built-in alarm time delay are useful for people who shift positions frequently during sleep. This system prevents the false alarms that can occur when people simply move on or off the pressure-sensor pads repeatedly. An alarm system that attaches to the bed or to the person is also useful under certain circumstances. For example, the weight of the person can be a factor. People who weigh under 100 pounds may not be able to apply sufficient weight to activate certain pressure-sensitive systems. In addition, antidecubiti pads added to the mattress may prevent the activation of some alarm systems.

All bed alarm systems, even when appropriately selected, raise some common concerns that need to be addressed: The efficacy of any alarm system is dependent on the response time of the nursing staff. One of the leading concerns of staff is that by the time the alarm sounds, staff may not be able to respond quickly enough to prevent a fall, particularly if the person's bedroom is located a considerable distance from the nurses' station. Other than attempting to relocate the person to a bedroom closer to the nurses' station, a solution to this problem is to make it difficult for the patient or resident to get out of bed. A decubiti-preventive water mattress filled to one half capacity, placed on the bed in combination with full-length bed side rails, is effective in limiting quick bed exits, even in the most agile person, and thus can provide nurses with adequate response time (Figure 5-14).

Skeptics contend that bed alarm systems are expensive both in terms of actual cost and manpower because additional nurses are needed to assist patients and residents. However, they are cost-effective in that they prevent falls and allow the staff to avoid using restraints. When measured against the costs of injuries sustained from bed falls and nursing time spent in caring for people recovering from the complications of falls and restraints, the cost of bed alarms are worthwhile. Most devices can be billed to diagnosis-related groups and to other third-party payers by charging a daily monitoring fee or budgeting the expense under the category "capital equipment." In addition, questions may be posed concerning legal liability and bed alarm use. Despite the use of these systems, the risk of bed falls and injuries continues. Although not challenged by the courts, hospitals and nursing facilities would do well to assume a defensive position in order to

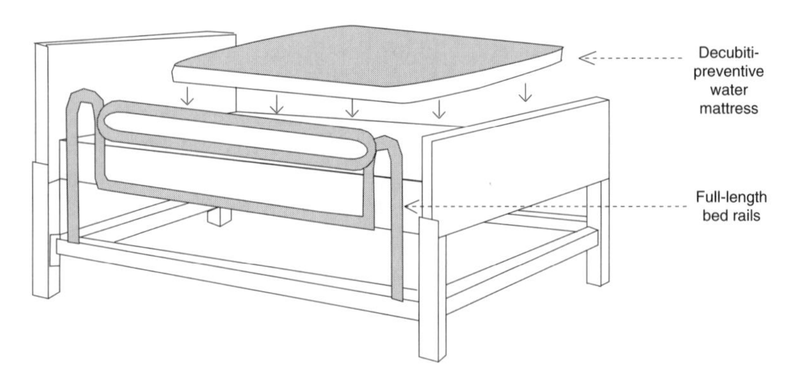

Figure 5-14. A bed with a water mattress prevents decubiti and full-length bed side rails prevent falls.

protect themselves. Assuming such a position would entail documenting the use of bed alarm devices in patients' or residents' charts as well as recording the rationale. Also, the risks and benefits of alarm systems should be explained to patients and residents, if competent, and family members; written consent should be obtained as well.

Legislation eliminating the use of mechanical restraints has contributed to a proliferation of bed alarm device manufacture. The result is healthy but confusing: healthy, because new and improved devices are introduced routinely; confusing, because the variety of choices makes it difficult to know which product to select. Bed alarm systems should meet a basic set of criteria:

- The system emits a distinctive alarm that is loud enough to be heard at the nurses' station and other locations.
- The system emits a silent alarm in the patient's or resident's bedroom and emits a loud alarm at the nurses' station so that sleeping patients or residents are not aroused by the alarm.
- The system has a built-in time delay, which reduces the number of false alarms.
- The system does not interfere with patient or resident care.
- The system is easy to use and maintain by staff.
- The system is durable; warranty and service contracts are included.

- The system has performed reliably and users, both nursing staff and patients or residents, are satisfied with the product. The customer should request a list of clients.

When purchasing the system, staff should ask the manufacturer whether its devices meet these standards.

Seating

Modification of chairs can be used to support independent and safe transfers in older adults with diminished transfer skills. Before seating can be modified, however, knowledge of seating standards is essential.

Seating Criteria

The criteria for proper seating in hospitals and nursing facilities is governed by one simple rule: Proper seating should meet the seating needs of patients and residents. To this end, chairs should assist in and not impede self-initiated transfers and provide comfort. Several methods are available to assess proper seating. Perhaps the most common is to select chairs that match the anthropometric, or body, measurements of older adults. For example

Seat height (Figure 5-15) is obtained by measuring a person's lower leg length, the distance from the foot on the floor to the

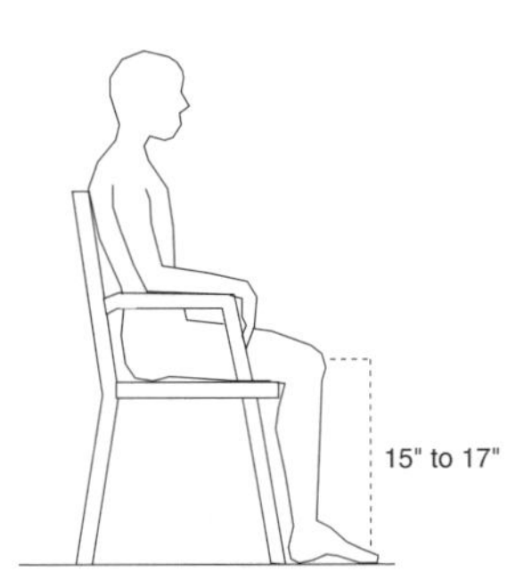

Figure 5-15. Seat height is appropriate when it is placed 15–17 inches from the floor.

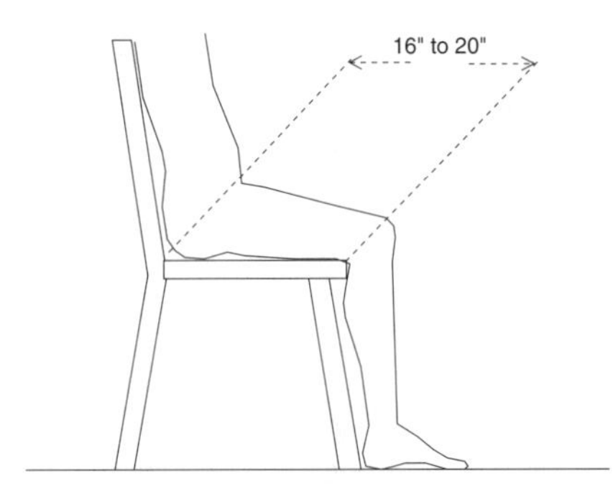

Figure 5-16. Seat depth is appropriate when it is located 16–20 inches from the popliteal area to the buttocks.

knee or popliteal area behind the knee—generally 15–17 inches.

Seat depth (Figure 5-16) is obtained by measuring upper leg length, the distance from the plane of the back to the popliteal area—generally 16 to 20 inches.

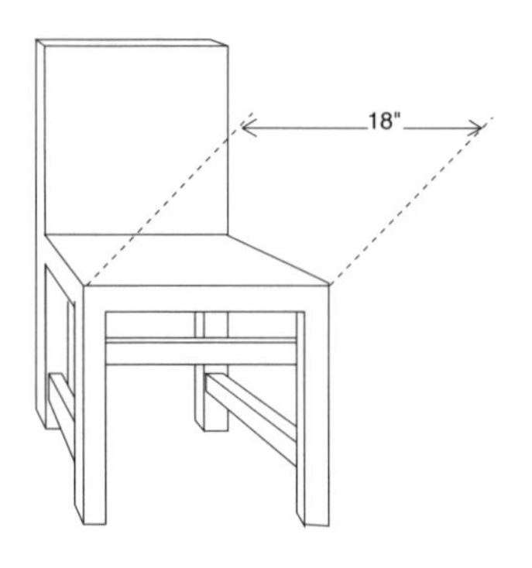

Figure 5-17. Seat width is appropriate when it is at least 18 inches wide.

Seat width (Figure 5-17) is obtained by measuring the distance across the widest point of the person's hips or thighs—generally 14 to 16 inches—and adding another 2 inches (i.e., 1 inch on each side of the hip) to prevent the body from rubbing or resting against the side of the chair.

The height of the armrest from the seat is generally 7–7½ inches.

The length of the armrest is generally 18–20 inches.

The seat slope is generally 7–10 inches.

The height of the backrest from the seat is generally 17 inches or higher.

Anthropometric seating criteria are useful for purchasing chairs in quantity, which is a common practice for most institutions because of the economic advantages offered. Appropriate seating requires more than simply selecting a chair or sofa that is anthropometrically correct, however. Even if these criteria are met, a person may experience problems with seating mobility. Therefore, the best method of assessing optimal seating is to observe the person actually using chairs in the environment to determine whether any difficulty is experienced. The individual performing the assessment must take into account the variability of individual anthropometric indices and the effects of different disease conditions as they affect chair mobility. The assessor must 1) watch the person sit down and rise from the chair and check that the task is performed safely and independently, and 2) ask whether the seat is comfortable when the person is seated.

Seat Height

Seat height, or the distance between the floor and the front edge of a chair, is critical to mobility. If the seat height is too low or too high, it can interfere with safe transfers. Seats that are too low require the body to move a great distance between sitting and standing positions: Greater knee flexion and leg muscle strength is necessary to initiate the upward thrust required to rise as well as support the downward motion needed to sit. This extra effort is especially hard on people whose range of motion in the knees and hips is limited and whose muscle strength is reduced. Conversely, it is much easier to transfer on and off higher-level seats. High-level seating requires the body to exert less joint flexion and muscle strength for both transfer functions.

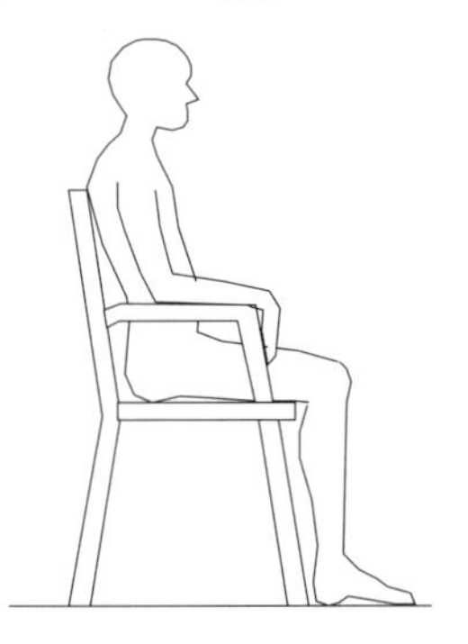

Figure 5-18. Seat height is appropriate when the person is able to sit with the knees flexed at 90° and both feet are planted firmly on the floor.

In an effort to compensate for low-level seating, people usually add either cushions or a pillow to the seat or select a higher chair on which to sit. However, compensation can be problematic. If the feet do not rest flat on the floor, the person is forced to slide from the seat to reach the floor when attempting to stand and to climb onto the seat when attempting to sit. Both movements can compromise safety. If loss of balance occurs, the person risks a fall. Seat height is appropriate when it allows the patient or resident to sit with both feet planted firmly on the floor and the knees flexed at 90° (Figure 5-18). The front of the seat should be low enough to allow for a small space between the thighs and the seat (Figure 5-19). The ability of another person to pass the flat of the hand freely underneath the seated person's

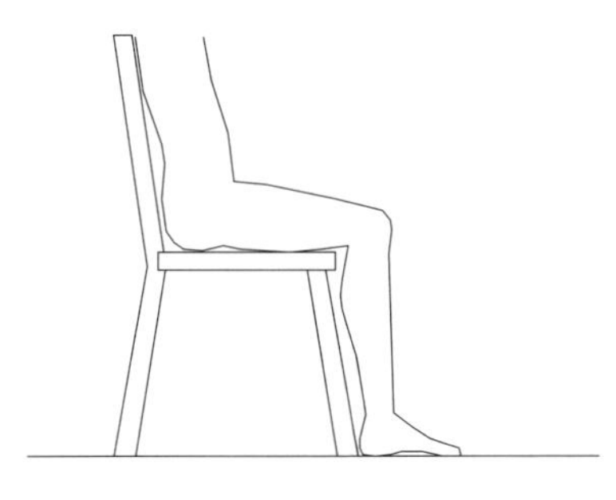

Figure 5-19. Front seat space.

thigh and edge of the seat provides a good index of the space that is required between the seat and the body. Low-level seating can be altered by providing patients and residents with chair seat heights that are functionally suited to the individual. If these heights are not available, a seating cushion can be added to the existing chair. Its width, or thickness, should be determined by how much height is needed to achieve independent mobility.

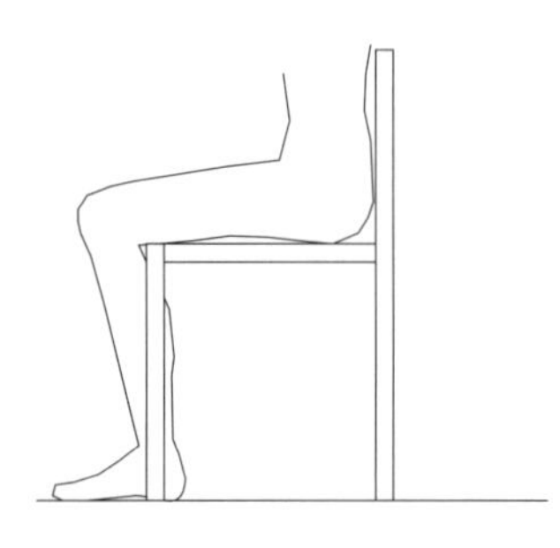

Figure 5-20. Leg kick space.

Leg Space

To facilitate rising from a chair, the provision of a kick space below a seat is essential (Figure 5-20). Proper kick space allows a person to slide one foot underneath the chair and one foot forward to obtain the leverage necessary for the lower extremities to exert maximum thrust upward. Cross-bars or cross-rails on chair legs, used to provide structural support, may interfere with rising if they are positioned too low or too far forward on the chair (Figure 5-21). Cross-bars or cross-rails should be positioned high enough or set back far enough to ensure that they do not interfere with the biomechanics of rising (Figure 5-22). The presence of armrests or seats that are somewhat higher may compensate for poorly positioned cross-rails.

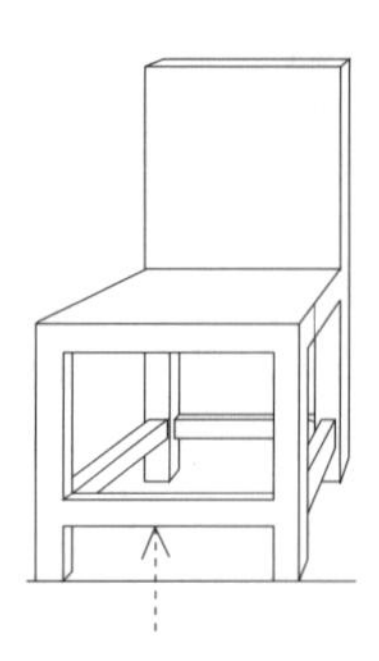

Figure 5-21. Cross-bars positioned too far forward or too low can interfere with safe rising from a seated position.

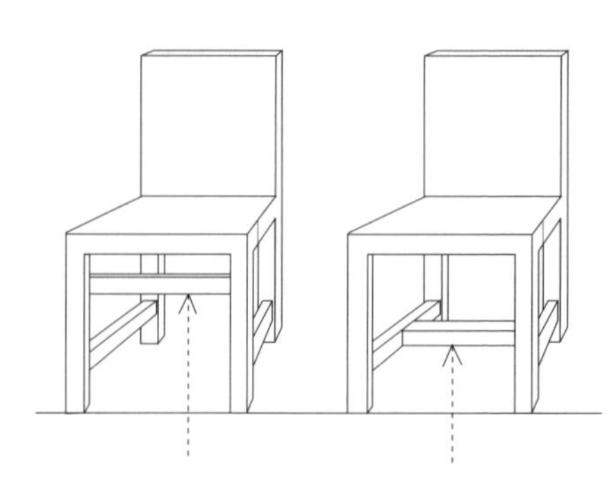

Figure 5-22. Appropriately positioned cross-bars.

Armrests

All chairs used by older people should be equipped with armrests. Older people, much more than younger people, depend on armrests for assistance in propelling body weight forward and maintaining balance when standing. The support offered by armrests while rising is additionally advantageous because it helps reduce pressure on the knee joints. Armrests also play a supportive role in helping a person to sit. A point is reached, particularly for individuals with decreased strength in the lower extremities or limited range of motion in the knees, when older adults' leg muscles and knee flexion no longer function effectively to help them sit down easily. As a result, they drop their body weight onto a seat. Armrests help arrest this quick, downward thrust of the body by assisting in its gradual descent.

Armrests that are too low, too high, or set back too far may inhibit both rising from the chair and sitting in it. Low-level armrests force a person to lean too far forward when rising and thus threaten balance. Armrests that are too high or set back too far cannot provide a sufficient angle of leverage for the upper extremities when rising from a seat (Figure 5-23). To achieve optimal function in providing assistance, armrests should be of the correct height, positioned horizontally 7–7½ inches above the seat (Figure 5-24). They should extend at least to the seat's edge or, ideally, 1 or 2 inches beyond the front edge (Figure 5-25). This position allows for maximum leverage when rising because it enables individuals to engage their stronger lower body muscles in the task of rising to a standing position, and continues to provide support until stability in standing is achieved (Figure 5-26). In addition, armrests should be nonslip; easy to grasp; and sloped slightly, more to the back than to the front, for maximum comfort.

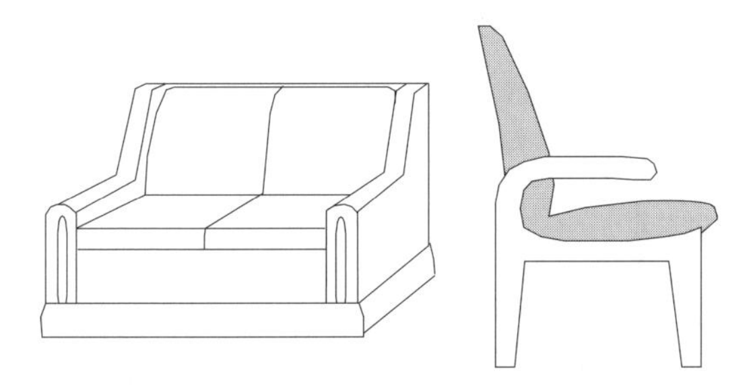

Figure 5-23. Nonsupportive armrest positions. (Left) Too low; (right) set back too far.

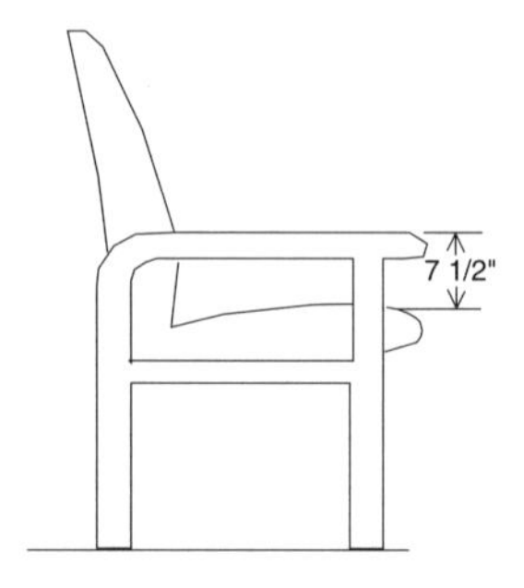

Figure 5-24. Appropriate armrest height.

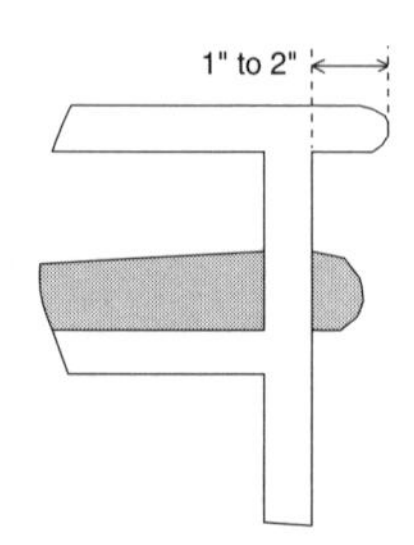

Figure 5-25. Appropriate armrest length.

Seat Depth and Backrest Angle

In general, the deeper the seat (i.e., the distance measured from the popliteal area to the buttocks), the greater the effort required of the person to move the body forward to the edge of the seat to rise. In addition to length, seat depth is affected by the angle of the backrest. The greater the angle or slant, the deeper the seat depth and the greater the distance a person must negotiate to pull him- or herself up (Figure 5-27).

The backrest or slope should always be considered in relation to the ability of the person to rise independently and should support the

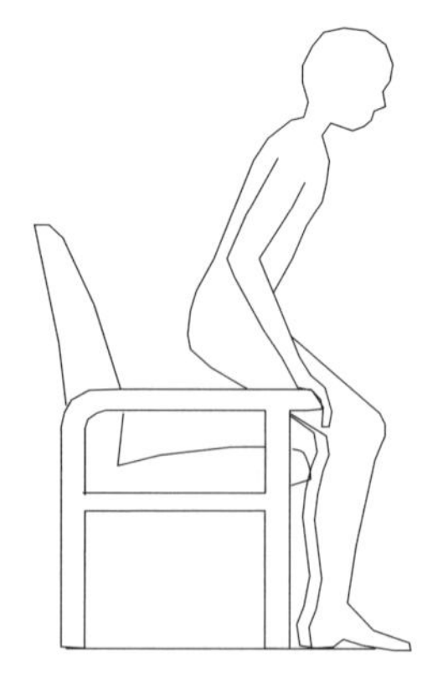

Figure 5-26. Armrest support during transfer activities.

Figure 5-27. Appropriate chair seat angle.

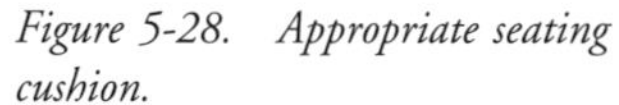

Figure 5-28. Appropriate seating cushion.

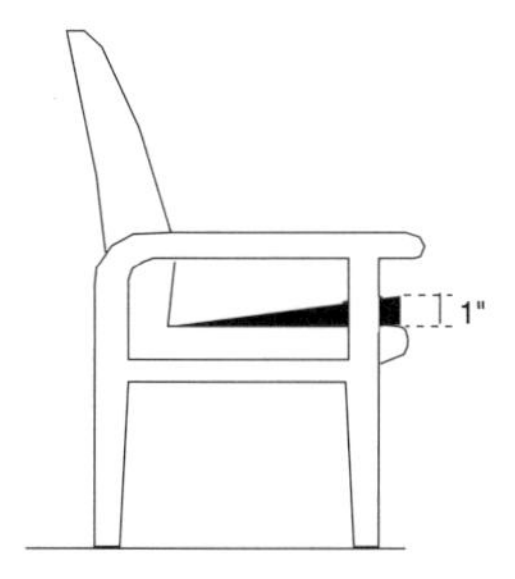

Figure 5-29. Appropriate angle for a seat slope.

lower back. If the seat is too deep or the angle of the backrest is too great, a seating cushion placed along the length of the backrest usually can correct the deficiency (Figure 5-28).

To facilitate rising from a chair, the seat should slope gently backward at an angle of no more than 1 inch from the front edge of the seat to its back edge (Figure 5-29). Seating that angles too far backward may present problems with rising because the person's knees will be positioned at a higher level than the buttocks (Figure 5-30). A seating angle that is tilted too far forward places the person's knees at a level that is lower than that of the buttocks and contributes to a slouched sitting position, which encourages sliding out of the chair (Figure 5-31). A wedge cushion can correct both problems (Figure 5-32). The

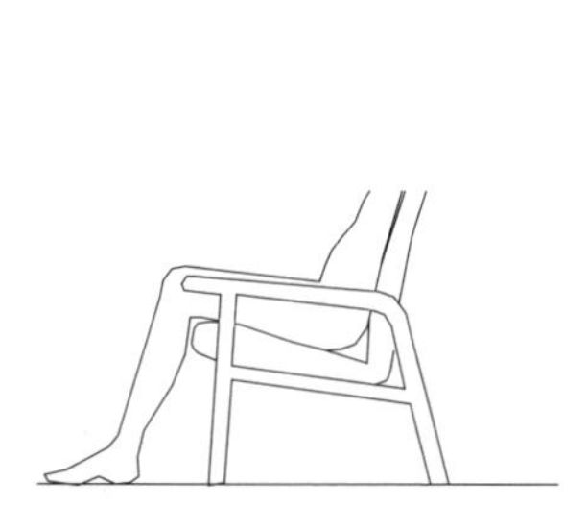

Figure 5-30. Appropriate backward seating angle.

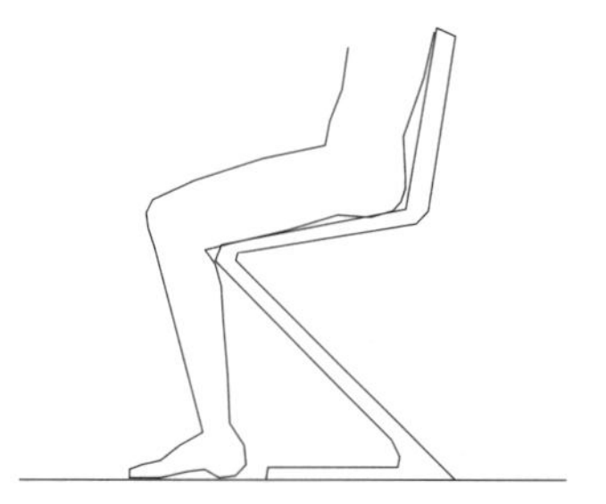

Figure 5-31. Appropriate forward seating angle.

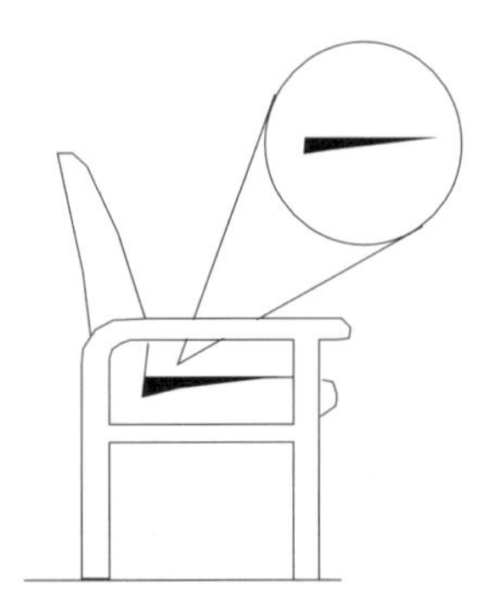

Figure 5-32. Appropriate wedged cushion.

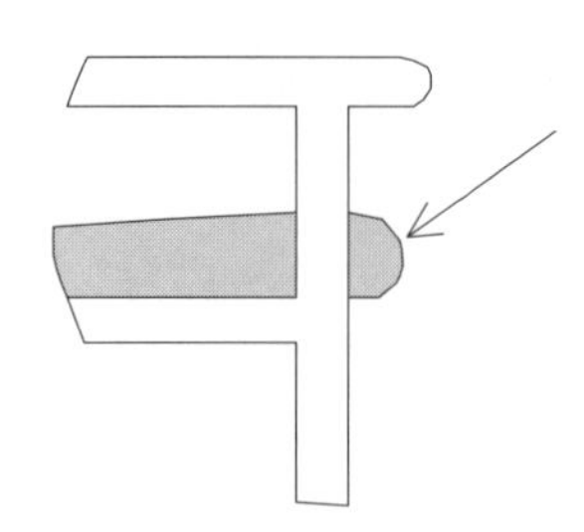

Figure 5-33. Appropriate curved seat edge.

wider part of the cushion should be positioned either at the front of the seat to prevent sliding or at the back to assist people who experience difficulty in rising from their seat. In addition, the front edge of the seat should curve gently to avoid placing pressure on the back of the person's knees (Figure 5-33), which restricts blood flow and causes the development of leg swelling or phlebitis.

Seating Cushions

Cushions on chairs should provide comfort and absorb the impact caused by a person sitting in a seat, but they should not be too soft. People tend to sink into overly soft cushions, making it difficult to get out of them. Moreover, overly soft cushions reduce effective seat height because they are compressed by the seated person, thus lowering the seat. As such, it is difficult to rise in one fluid motion. Also, overly soft cushions prevent people from shifting their buttocks, a natural and protective motion that helps individuals to avoid developing decubiti.

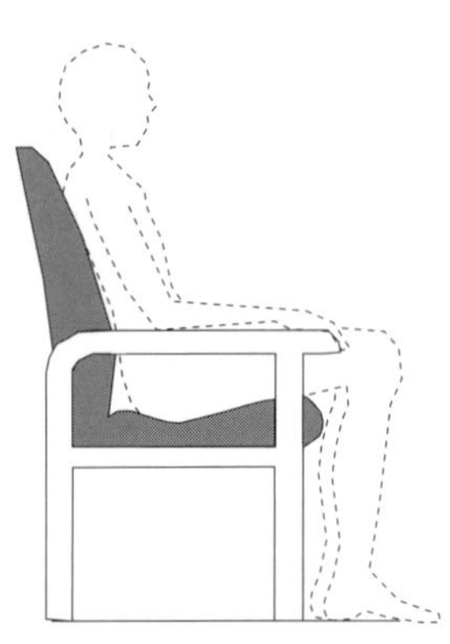

Figure 5-34. Appropriate soft seat cushion.

The best type of seating cushion for chairs is one that is relatively flat and firm, has some resilience, and does not "bottom out" when a person sits on it (Figure 5-34). A suitable cushion should give way when a fist is pressed firmly into it, yet resist if further pressure is applied. A cushion consisting of latex material provides pliancy sufficient for comfort and firmness, without excessive compression. Foam cushions should be avoided because they lose resilience over time and tend to bottom out. The color of the seat cushion should contrast that of the chair so that it can be seen during seating. To prevent sliding, the seat covering should be manufactured of a slip-resistant material.

Seating Stability

The stability of a chair is crucial to a person's safety. If, during the act of transferring, the chair tips forward, sideways, or backward, the risk of loss of balance and falling is increased greatly. Chairs with a seat edge that significantly overhangs the position of the legs should be avoided. This design can cause the chair to tip forward when a person moves to its front edge to rise or sits on the edge rather than in the middle of the seat (Figure 5-35). Casters or metal tips attached to the ends of the chair legs can be dangerous, especially on slick linoleum flooring. The weight of the body can cause chairs that are equipped with these devices to slide when the person sits, rises, or leans on the chair for balance support. Dining room chairs, in particular, can be precarious. Although dining chairs must pull away easily from the table, casters are too unstable for most frail older people to use safely. In general, casters and metal tips should be removed. As an alternative, chairs can be placed up against the wall, which prevents them from sliding away during transfers.

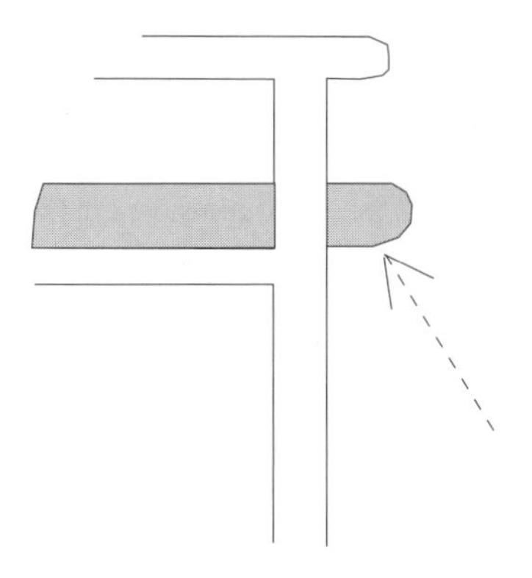

Figure 5-35. Appropriate elongated seat cushion.

Chairs are most stable when the chair legs are straight, positioned well forward of the seat's leading edge but not so splayed as to invite tripping, and the edge of the seat does not extend too far forward beyond the chair legs. In addition, some individuals with balance problems use chair backrests for mobility support. Thus, backrests should be placed high enough on the chair in order to provide adequate support. In general, a height of approximately 32 inches, the distance from the floor to the top of the backrest, is sufficient for this purpose (Figure 5-36). The backrest must be nonslip for safe grasping: A nonslip adhesive strip placed along the backrest prevents slipping. A good test of a chair's stability is for a staff member to grasp and lean into a chair, and slide and tilt it forward, backward, and sideways.

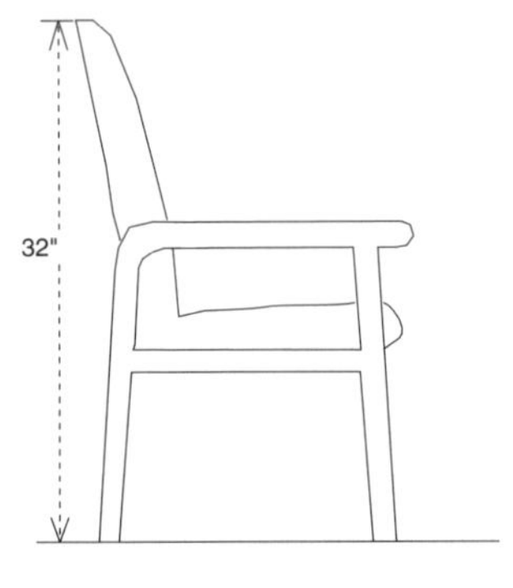

Figure 5-36. Appropriate backrest height.

Seating Alternatives to Restraints

Patients and residents who experience poor mobility and remain at fall risk, despite the adaptation of existing chairs, may benefit from one of several different types of seats. A deep-seated, soft-cushioned lounge chair or recliner with a seat that slants downward toward the back; a wedge cushion, the widest part of which is placed toward the front of the seat (Figure 5-37); or a beanbag chair filled with Styrofoam pellets may be alternatives to mechanical restraints. These furnishings work by keeping an individual's buttocks at a level that is lower than that of the knees, making it exceedingly difficult for the person to rise. Their purpose is to prevent the person who cannot ambulate safely from getting up independently or from sliding off a seat. Caution is advised because this seating position places increased pressure on the buttocks, particularly on the buttocks of thin individuals, placing them at risk for developing decubiti. Although these seats are considered by some critics to be restraints because they prevent independent movement, they can help people avoid many of the harmful effects associated with mechanical restraints (see Chapter 6).

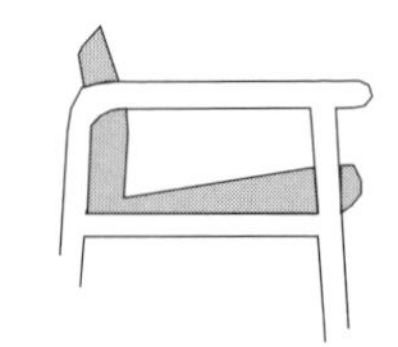

Figure 5-37. A seat that slants backward prevents independent rising.

If these seating choices are unsuitable, a chair alarm system may serve as an option. A chair alarm system is a battery-powered portable device that consists of either a cord that attaches to the person's gown or a pressure-sensitive pad that rests on the seat or against the backrest. When a patient or resident slides to the edge of the chair or attempts to stand, the device sounds an alarm that alerts the nursing staff. The indications for a chair alarm are as follows:

- Patient or resident experiences fall(s) from a chair or wheelchair
- Patient or resident experiences fall(s) while ambulating (shortly after rising from the chair) or is found on the floor next to the chair or wheelchair (unwitnessed fall)
- Patient or resident demonstrates unsafe chair/wheelchair transfers
- Patient or resident has a history of cognitive or communication problems (e.g., forgets to ask for assistance with chair transfers)

Chair alarms are effective, but only to a point. By the time a nurse comes to assist a patient or resident, the person already may be standing or he or she may be lying on the floor. Placing pressure-sensitive pads against the chair backrest and keeping the length of clothing-attached cords short helps staff detect early departure from chairs. In order to be heard by staff, chair alarms are generally loud, which can have a negative impact on patients and residents (e.g., the loud sound may frighten them) and lead to a fear of leaving the chair.

Bathroom

For older adults with poor walking and transferring balance, bathrooms can be especially hazardous places. Modifications of the existing bathroom can help to support safe mobility and reduce the risk of falls and injury.

Fixture Support

Patients and residents with balance dysfunction and people who are unable to use their walkers in the bathroom because of space limita-

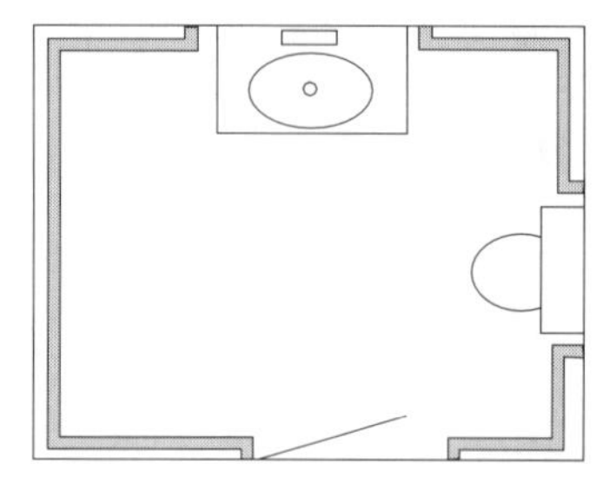

Figure 5-38. Bathroom grab rails.

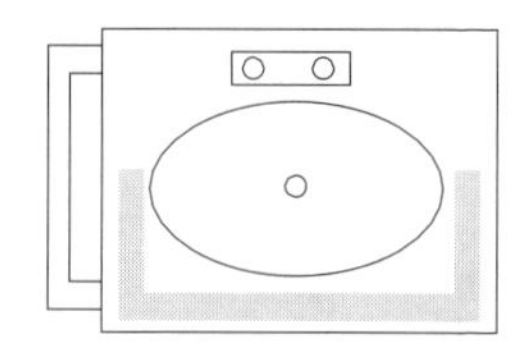

Figure 5-39. Nonslip adhesive strips placed on a sink.

tions often resort to the use of sink tops, towel bars, and wall surfaces for support. These structures are poor alternatives and may contribute to falls, particularly if the individual's hand slips. Moreover, towel bars are often located too high on the wall to provide adequate support. Several modifications to eliminate this hazard are available: A grab bar placed horizontally in place of the towel bar or a grab rail that runs around the perimeter of the bathroom wall can be used to provide balance support (Figure 5-38).

The color of the grab bars should contrast that of the wall for visibility, be slip-resistant (vinyl coating offers a better gripping surface than do standard metal bars), and be positioned no more than 1½ inches from the wall to keep a person's arm from slipping between the bar and the wall. It is important that grab bars are attached securely to wall studs so that they do not give way easily. A wide variety of grab bar lengths and angles are available, which allows health care providers to tailor grab bars to specific patient and resident needs.

Nonslip adhesive strips placed along sinktops prevent hands from sliding (Figure 5-39). The color of the strips should be similar to that of the sink top to eliminate visual confusion. In addition, grab bars can be mounted on the face of vanity tops to provide an additional support surface.

Toilets

Toilets that are low in height often cause problems in transferring. To circumvent such problems, corrective modifications should be made, which can include raised toilet seats and grab bars. Raised toilet seats are available in two types: fixed and adjustable height. The latter are preferable because they can be easily adjusted to provide the proper sitting height. Several sizes of fixed-height toilet seats should be available to accommodate individual needs. It is advised that raised toilet seats be constructed of materials that are sturdy enough to provide support. The seats themselves should be made of a soft vinyl or plastic to provide patients or residents with an absorptive cushion. An absorptive cushion reduces the risk of pelvic or hip fracture in people who have a tendency to drop onto the toilet seat. The color of the toilet seat should contrast that of the toilet tank and bowl and surrounding area to facilitate individuals' proper seating placement, particularly in people who depend on visual cueing. Contrasting the color of bathroom walls with that of the toilet can help people to visualize the toilet as well.

The installation of grab bars on the wall next to and behind the toilet or a double armrest grab bar system, commonly referred to as a toilet safety frame, that attaches to the toilet can be used by patients and residents to maintain their balance during toilet transfers. The type and height placement of grab bars mounted to walls depends on the individual, his or her disability, and the surrounding environment. For example, people with hemiplegia find it difficult to use grab bars placed on their dysfunctional side, people of short stature or limited reach find grab bars placed at heights that are convenient for the "average person" unsatisfactory because they are beyond their reach, and people in wheelchairs experience transfer problems with conventional grab bars and find wall-mounted "swing-up" or "hinged-arm" grab bars easier to use. (This type of grab bar folds flat against the wall directly behind the toilet when not in use and can be moved to the horizontal position when in use.)

An alternative to wall-mounted grab bars is the toilet safety frame, or double armrest system (Figure 5-40). Many older people find this grab bar easier to use because the maximum amount of force exerted during transfers is completed in a straight-downward movement of the arms, which provides optimum transferring support. Conversely, wall-mounted grab bars provide less support because, when transferring, the person must reach to the side and bend forward in order to grab the bar. As a result, the direct benefit of a downward thrust offered by the double armrest system is lost. The double armrest

Figure 5-40. Toilet safety frame.

system is convenient for staff because it is easy to attach and can be readily adjusted for an individual patient or resident. As a cautionary measure, nonslip adhesive strips in a noncontrasting color should be placed on the floor in front of the toilet to prevent the person's feet from slipping during transfers. Nurse call alarms located in the bathroom and toilet paper holders must be accessible to guard against falls from the toilet.

Patients and residents who are unable to toilet autonomously, such as older adults with ambulation and/or transfer problems and with a bathroom that is located a considerable distance from the bed, may be able to maintain independence by using a bedside commode. Bedside commodes that are height adjustable for individual variation and fitted with armrest support to facilitate safe transfers should be chosen. Commodes that are equipped with wheels should be avoided because they can roll away easily during transfers.

Tables and Nightstands

Many patients and residents with balance disorders use the edges of tabletops and nightstands for transferring and walking support. If these furnishings are unstable or the tops are slippery when grasped, they may fail to provide balance support. Furnishings that are not supportive can cause individuals to develop a fear of falling as well. It is best to avoid pedestal-style tables, which tend to tip over easily when a person's weight is applied to the edge (Figure 5-41). Nightstands that are used to assist with bed transfers may slide away, particularly if they are equipped with wheels or metal casters. Over-the-bed tables are similarly dangerous.

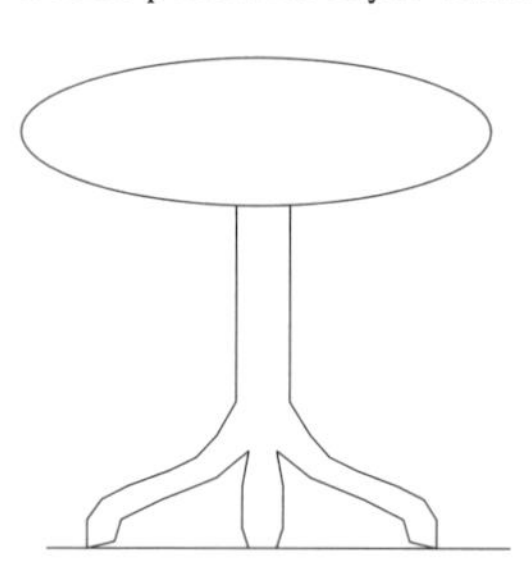

Figure 5-41. Pedestal table.

All tables and nightstands in the institutional environment should be stable when leaned on or grasped. They should have nonslip surfaces. Stability can be achieved by selecting tables with four legs that are free of wheels or casters and have a slip-resistant matte surface that promotes grasping. Tabletops with a contrasting border help patients and residents identify the boundary of the table, thus promoting proper hand placement and support and averting "bumping into" accidents. Table edges that are rounded or bullnosed prevent bumping injuries that result from contact with sharp edges. Dining tables with spill-free edges, which restrain spilled liquids, are useful because they guard against wet floors and slippage. Dining room tables and chairs should work together: The arms of chairs and wheelchairs should fit under the table to allow older people to move in as close as possible for dining and avoid fluid spillage. To accommodate wheelchairs, tables must be approximately 34 inches high. Because this height may be excessive for people dining in regular chairs, tables with adjustable height bases to accommodate both populations should be purchased. In addition, the position of tables and nightstands in the institutional environment should not obstruct ambulation.

Storage Areas

All closets and dressers used by patients and residents must be accessible without the need for excessive reaching or bending. Frequently used items such as day and night wear and footwear should be placed on shelves or in drawers that lie between the person's eye and waist levels. This height accommodates the functional reach of most older people, thus minimizing the risk of balance loss.

Notes

[1]Healey, F. (1994). Does flooring type affect risk of injury in older in-patients? *Nursing Times*, 90(27), 40–41.

[2]*Fixed Low Beds*: Model 833 AG (5 1/2 inches in height), Gem Industries, Inc., Phone (706) 886-8431; ONYX (7 inches in height), NoaMedical, Phone (888) 662-6699. *Hi-Low Beds*: NoaRiser (7–23 inches in height), NoaMedical; Volker (17–23 inches in height; features integrated bed side rails that disappear when not in use and disappearing casters), Hertz Supply Company, Inc., Phone (800) 321-4240; Model H-3135-75/80 LF (15–24 1/4 inches in height), Gem Industries, Inc. (15–24 inches in height).

[3]Available from Distinct Medical Supplies, Ltd., 9 Commercial Plaza, Elkton, Maryland 21921. Phone (410) 398-0555.

[4]Heslin, K., Towers, J., Lecki, C., et al. (1992). Managing falls: Identifying population-specific risk factors and preventive strategies. In S.G. Funk, E.M. Tornquist, M.T. Champage, & R.A. Wiese (Eds.), *Key aspects of elder care: Managing falls, incontinence, and cognitive impairment* (pp. 70–88). New York: Springer.

[5]Widder, B. (1985). A new device to decrease falls. *Geriatric Nursing*, 6, 287–288.

chapter six

Reducing Mechanical and Chemical Restraints

Until the 1990s, the sight of an old, frail person being restrained to a bed or chair was a familiar scene in hospitals and nursing facilities throughout the United States. Anywhere from 25% to 85% of older adults—more than half a million individuals—in these institutions were placed in mechanical restraints each day.[1] Concern about their lack of effectiveness, safety, and serious consequences has been growing in the U.S. health care community and among sensitive laypeople. Some of the concern also derives from the fact that restraints are little used in European long-term care facilities. As a result, a nationwide effort is underway to reduce and, eventually, eliminate the use of restraints as a fall prevention measure. The impetus stems from consumer advocates, health professionals, and government regulators who are concerned that mechanical restraints have become routine, acceptable forms of treatment. Opponents argue that in many institutions, restraints represent the standard approach to common problems of old age such as falls and conditions associated with fall risk such as mobility dysfunction and confusion. They posit that criteria governing the use of restraints are lacking and that decisions to restrain are seldom documented or challenged; for the most part, restraints are sanctioned by institution administration to comply with directives to maintain "safe" practice. In addition, opponents point out that efforts to remove restraints are infrequent and alternatives to their use rarely explored. In general, once applied to an individual, restraints are permanent. As a result, policies aimed at the elimination of mechanical restraints are beginning to be developed. The most prominent policy is the Omnibus Budget Reconciliation Act (OBRA), enacted by the federal government in 1987. OBRA represents a legislative concern about the quality of care in nursing facilities in general and the widespread use of restraints in particular. Implemented in 1990, one of OBRA's strongest mandates is that nursing facilities examine their use of mechanical restraints and begin to find alternatives. As a consequence of OBRA regulations, the use of restraints in nursing facilities has declined dramatically, from a prevalence rate of 41% in 1988 to 22% in 1992—nearly a 47% decrease. The movement to reduce restraints has affected acute care hospitals as well. Modeled after OBRA, restraint-reduction initiatives for hospitals have been put into place by the Joint Commission on Accreditation of Healthcare Organizations.

RATIONALE

The reasons for the use of mechanical restraints in hospitals and nursing facilities are often multifactorial, encompassing both patient and resident, or host-related, and institutional factors:[2]

- Patient/resident-related factors
  - Prevent falls and related injury
  - Decrease fall risk resulting from mobility problems, unsafe wandering, confusion, or agitated behaviors
  - Correct seating alignment
- Institutional factors
  - Frail patients and residents are at risk for falls, injury, or both if not restrained
  - Inadequate staffing requires the use of restraints

Institutions have a "moral duty" to protect patients and residents
Failure to restrain places employees and the facility at legal risk
Restraints allow nurses to provide efficient and timely care
Families request and demand "risk-free" care, which includes restraint use
Few alternatives to restraints exist

Although restraints are designed to protect patients and residents from falls and harm, they are not the best choice, nor do they represent the best solution, except possibly under extreme circumstances. As mentioned in the list, all of the firmly entrenched beliefs that support their continued use are based on myth because no documented evidence exists that restraints are effective in accomplishing the purposes for which they are used. Many studies conclude that restraints seldom eliminate the risk of injury from falls but that, conversely, they can precipitate or exacerbate the problem. Most researchers concur that people in restraints are subject to the same or added fall risk as are individuals without restraints. Among facilities that do or do not use restraints, little difference exists in the extent of fall occurrences.[3] Moreover, facilities that do restrain experience a higher incidence of serious injury following falls.[4] When restraints are removed, there may be an increase in the number of falls, but not in the number that result in significant injury.

Some nurses believe that rendering care to patients and residents is easier and more efficient when restraints are used. Although it may appear that providing daily care to people with mobility problems is achieved more quickly when they are restrained, this strategy is ineffective. People in restraints rapidly develop immobility and associated morbidity, which creates greater dependency and need for custodial care from the staff and heightens the risk of falls. Aside from concerns about effectiveness, the use of restraints to "protect and safeguard" patients and residents is suspect. Although restraints have been applied in some instances for protective reasons (e.g., to prevent falls in people who are confused and wander when an immediate and clear threat of injury exists), the risks associated with restraints outweigh the benefits. The arguments supporting restraint use in protecting patients and residents at risk for immediate harm are questionable because alternatives such as beanbag chairs serve the same purpose and do not subject them to harm.

Rather than protecting older adults, restraints place them at risk for numerous detrimental physical and psychological consequences. Restraints that are too restrictive or applied too tightly can cause circulatory obstruction of the lower extremities, edema, skin abrasions, respiratory difficulties, and unintentional death by strangulation. Hospital patients who are restrained have twice the length of institutional stay of those who are free from restraints; they are also more likely to be transferred to nursing facilities for care and are at higher risk for early death. Much of the resulting mortality is the consequence of restraint use and its concomitant immobility.

The psychological consequences of restraints are many and help refute any beliefs that older people are not bothered by their use. Often, application triggers one of several emotional reactions: People feel either fear and a sense of panic, which can result in belligerent behavior, or a sense of humiliation and abandonment, which can result in aggressive behavior, a loss of self-image, depression, withdrawal, or low social functioning. In addition, self-esteem decreases because, typically, others view individuals who are in restraints as disturbed, dangerous, or mentally incompetent, which can be demoralizing. Moreover, when older adults are not informed about the decision to apply restraints or are not allowed to either accept or refuse their use, they are denied their right of self-determination. This violation of personal rights constitutes a restriction of an individual's autonomy, the freedom to make choices about engaging in activities. When a person is restrained and denied the ability to get up, sit down, or walk about with undue interference, his or her quality of life and psychological well-being are impaired.

Health care professionals are not immune from the effects of restraints. Nurses, who are often responsible for initiating restraint orders in hospitals and nursing facilities, struggle with the burden brought on by this decision. On the one hand, they feel a professional duty to protect and safeguard people who are at risk for falls. This obligation is often heightened when nursing allocations are scarce and monitoring of problematic individuals is difficult. To avoid the risk of legal sanctions, some nurses feel that they have no alternative but to apply restraints. On the other hand, nurses find the act of restraining older people stressful and emotionally taxing, often provoking anxiety, dissatisfaction, and guilt in them. They recognize that restraints deprive individuals of their autonomy and dignity, and they sympathize with them, conceding that they themselves would not want to be placed in a similar position.

Although nurses perceive themselves as less vulnerable to legal sanctions if restraints are used, particularly in the event of injury, the fear of legal liability is ill-founded. Despite the fact that lawsuits for damages resulting from falls are relatively common, few have been successful against facilities and their employees solely for the failure to restrain. In cases involving injury to people without restraints, a preponderance of other factors usually constitutes negligence, including improper assessment and documentation of the patient's or resident's condition, failure to assess and monitor the person at risk for falls, and failure to respond to falls and injury in a timely manner. Rather, the use of restraints may increase the risk of litigation. Lawsuits involving the improper application of restraints that results in patient and resident injury (e.g., falling out of a bed or chair either with restraints intact or removed by the person) have been successful. In addition, facilities and staff may be held liable when restraints are used for convenience, for example, during staffing shortages.

Family members are also affected by restraint decisions and react in various ways to finding their relative restrained. Some express dismay at the sight of a relative in restraints and demand their removal, even if the action places the person at fall risk. Others, although not accepting of the practice, come to accept restraints as a necessary evil, believing that they will keep their relative from being injured in a fall. This notion is reinforced when family members are not informed by staff of the harmful effects of restraints and of the available alternatives for safeguarding their relative.

Much of the justification for using mechanical and chemical restraints is based on the misapprehension that no alternatives are available. Many hospitals and nursing facilities in the United States have deliberately reduced restraint use without experiencing a concomitant rise in serious injury. Such facilities have adopted a policy of nonrestraint use that is employed commonly in several European countries. These countries place greater emphasis on structuring the physical environment and the activities of patients and residents in such a way that restraints are rarely, if ever, needed or used.

Management

The challenge for health care professionals in hospitals and nursing facilities is reducing the use of mechanical and chemical restraints while decreasing the risk of falls. To achieve this objective, hospital and nursing facility staff can take a number of steps within their individual facilities:

Step 1—Examine current restraint practices, the attitudes of employees toward their use, and institutional policies that govern the use of mechanical and chemical restraints. The intent of this exercise is to determine the prevalence of restraint use; the availability, utilization, and effectiveness of restraint alternatives; and whether policies are viable and provide staff with appropriate direction in the use of restraints. Inquire about the following:

- To what extent are restraints used?
- Under what circumstances or conditions are restraints ordered and why?
- Are restraints the first or last choice in treatment?
- Are restraints effective in controlling the risk of falls?
- Are restraints used continuously, intermittently, or on a short-term basis? Under what conditions?
- Are patients and residents (if able) and family members consulted on the need for restraints and given the right of refusal?
- If either party refuses the use of restraints, what procedures are in place to ensure the patient's or resident's safety?
- Are individuals who are restrained observed or monitored for nutritional or toileting needs and adverse effects? How often? By whom?
- If individuals experience adverse effects, are restraints discontinued? If not, why? If so, what forms of management are used to replace restraints?
- Are restraint alternatives ever considered as an initial choice of treatment? Under what circumstances?
- What types of alternative treatments are available? Are they effective in controlling the problem indicated? If not, why?
- Are institutional policies clear as to the types of conditions or situations in which restraints can and cannot be used; the

types of restraint alternatives available; the assessment procedure for restraint use and discontinuation; and who has the responsibility of ordering, monitoring, and documenting restraint and nonrestraint use?
- Are institutional policies updated periodically? Are staff members aware of the content in policy statements?

Step 2—Establish an ongoing program of in-service education aimed at assessing restraints (see the exhibit on p. 132) and assessing and managing the problems (e.g., dysmobility, falls, confusion, wandering, poor sitting posture) that are cited commonly as indications for restraints. These problems should not be viewed as end-stage processes but as signs of an underlying medical or environmental condition. Ordering a restraint as initial treatment is inappropriate; rather, these problems should trigger further investigation and treatment aimed at eliminating the underlying conditions responsible. If the problem persists, alternatives to the use of restraints should be explored (see the exhibit on p. 133). Restraints, if necessary, should be considered only as a temporary measure to be used under extreme emergency conditions or as a last resort when the advantages to the patient or resident clearly outweigh the disadvantages. To this end, attention to staff education regarding selection of appropriate restraints and their proper application is warranted. In general, the restraint chosen should be the one that is the least restrictive and safest. Both the patient or resident and the restraint should be checked frequently.

Step 3—Hospitals and nursing facilities should develop and implement restraint-reduction policies. The purpose of these policies is to provide staff with step-by-step guidelines related to mechanical restraint decisions and care for patients and residents. These documents also can serve as defense against potential legal liability because they illustrate an attempt by the institution and staff to practice reasonable standards of restraint practice. The policy statement should be clear and simple to follow and address the following points specifically:

- Define what a mechanical restraint is and describe the types of restraining devices available.
- Define and categorize the types of situations in which restraints may or may not be used.
- Define the assessment procedure for the application and discontinuation of restraints.

Content for Educational In-Service on Restraints

I. Overview of restraints
   A. Prevalence
   B. Reasons for restraints
      1. Avoidance of falls
      2. Control of wandering behavior
      3. Control of agitation/behavior problems
      4. Correction of seating/positioning problems
   C. Ineffectiveness of restraints in managing patient or resident safety

II. Adverse effects of restraints
   A. Physiological consequences
   B. Loss of autonomy
   C. Loss of dignity
   D. Agitation/depression
   E. Family and staff discomfort

III. Legal
   A. Current OBRA and JCAHO regulations concerning restraint use
   B. Institutional policies regarding restraints
   C. Staff liability issues

IV. Restraint alternatives
   A. Assessment
      1. Identify causes of fall risk
      2. Identify causes of wandering
      3. Identify causes of agitation/behavior problems
      4. Identify causes of seating problems
   B. Nonrestraint management
      1. Modify underlying problems discovered
         a. Fall risk
         b. Wandering
         c. Agitation/behavior manifestations
         d. Poor seating
      2. Review available restraint alternatives
         a. Approaches/methods to support seating
         b. Approaches/methods to guard against falls
         c. Approaches/methods to permit safe wandering
         d. Approaches/methods to manage behavior manifestations
         e. Approaches/methods to support mobility

Alternatives to Restraints

Caregiving

Additional nursing supervision/observation of activities
Assistance of family members/volunteers (companionship, supervision of activities)
Daily ambulation, structured activities
Exercise; gait/balance training
Instruction on safe chair/wheelchair transfers
Maintain regular toileting schedule
Evaluate adverse medication affects
Correct sensory deficits (e.g., eyeglasses, hearing aids)
Provide safety when patient or resident judgment is impaired

Environmental

Orient patient/resident to environment
Arrange for patient/resident to be near nurses' station
Provide adequate lighting, night-lights
Maintain obstacle-free environment
Provide ambulation devices
Employ strategic seating
Make available a variety of seating options (different heights, seat angles)
Provide alternative seating (wedge cushions, seating props, slanting chairs, beanbag chairs)
Provide nonslip floor surfaces
Supply/encourage appropriate footwear
Provide bed and chair alarms, accessible call buttons
Lower bed height, mattress on floor
Remove bed wheels
Provide accessible call light
Avoid full-length bed side rails
Use half bed side rails to support transfers ("enablers")
Provide commode at bedside
Provide perimeter alarms, safe wandering areas
Provide Merry Walker (designed walker that permits independent ambulation for individuals with dementia or confusion)

- Define who has the responsibility for ordering and discontinuing restraints.
- Define the procedure and staff responsibilities for documenting restraint use.
- Define the procedure for monitoring restraint use.
- Define the types of circumstances under which restraint alternatives should be considered.
- Define the types of restraint alternatives available.
- Define the procedure to follow when patients and residents or family members refuse restraints.
- Define a procedure for ensuring that all staff are aware of the institution's policy and that the contents of the policy are updated periodically.

Reducing mechanical restraints may be difficult to achieve in all instances, and perhaps more so in the acute care hospital than in the nursing facility setting. It is important to recognize that, with respect to fall-prevention efforts, "good" care consists of helping patients and residents to achieve maximum independence while attempting to reduce the likelihood of falls. It is clear that there are few justifications for the use of mechanical restraints and that restraints are more likely to cause falls than prevent them.

Health care providers also must be cognizant of chemical restraints—the misuse of psychoactive medications—and eliminate this practice. The most common categories of psychoactive medications include antipsychotics (i.e., neuroleptics or major tranquilizers), anxiolytics (i.e., antianxiety or minor tranquilizers), sedatives and hypnotics (i.e., sleep inducers), and antidepressants. Often, these drugs are prescribed to control mood, mental status, or behavior—acute confusional states, agitated or violent behaviors, anxiety, depressive states, wandering—that places patients and residents at risk for falls or other harmful consequences. Inappropriate use of chemical restraints consists of the following:

- Given without specific indications
- Prescribed in excessive dosages, which affect an older adult's ability to function properly
- Used as sole treatment without investigating alternative nonpharmacological or behavioral interventions

- Administered for purposes of discipline or convenience of the staff

Many cases of inappropriate psychoactive drug use result from the mistaken belief that these medications represent the only way of managing behaviors or from the fact that they are used as a substitute for adequate treatment.

Whether psychoactive medications are used as therapeutic agents or as restraints may be difficult to determine. For example, a psychoactive drug may be prescribed to treat agitated behavior, and its use results in an increased fall risk. The psychoactive drug is considered a therapeutic agent if it controls the individual's behavior and eliminates the risk of falls without restricting his or her ability to function; it is deemed a restraint if the person's activities (e.g., getting out of bed, going to the bathroom, engaging in social activities) are inhibited. Other medications used by older adults may be considered to be chemical restraints. For instance, some medications prescribed for physical ailments such as nonsteroidal anti-inflammatory drugs (analgesics), antihypertensives, and cardiotonics (cardiac drugs) can produce side effects such as disorientation, confusion, dizziness, and orthostatic hypotension or low blood pressure. In addition, polypharmacy (i.e., taking five or more medications) is common among older people. Any adverse interactions between drugs such as increased sedation or loss of coordination can result in cognitive and mobility impairments.

Aside from chemical restraints, the side effects of psychoactive drugs are particularly taxing on the physiological systems of older people. These side effects may include increased drowsiness, delirium or disordered thinking, low blood pressure, and Parkinsonian symptoms such as muscle rigidity in the limbs and gait disturbances. Such conditions may not only lead to further disruptive behavior but also increase the risk of falls and hip fractures. Also, psychoactive drugs may produce paradoxical agitation (i.e., rather than calming down a person, the drugs can sometimes increase agitation) in some older individuals, which clouds the issue of whether to increase or decrease drug dosages. Any increase of medication is likely to result in a vicious cycle of higher doses and decreased functional ability.

Health care providers must take several steps before using psychoactive medications in patients and residents who present with cognitive disturbances, behavior disturbances, or both: Identify the disturbance or specific symptom, and, if possible, discover the cause of the disturbance. Assessment of the underlying conditions responsible may eliminate the need for psychoactive medications. For example, confusion leading to disoriented behavior, agitation, or falling episodes may be due to an underlying infection or pharmacotoxicity. Thus, giving an antibiotic to clear the infection or stopping the medication is more appropriate than giving a psychoactive. Other common causes of disturbed behavior and changes in cognitive function in older people are the presence of pain, fecal impaction, metabolic abnormalities, and acute exasperation of chronic diseases. Also, simple events such as a wet bed, a room that is too hot or too cold, and hunger or thirst should not be overlooked as causes of behavior disturbances. Attempts should be made to reverse or eliminate the underlying cause through nonpharmacological approaches. In many instances, intervention with corrective behavioral and/or environmental strategies eliminates the need for psychoactive drugs. For instance, a succession of stressful events such as declining health, episodes of falling, admission to a hospital or a nursing facility, and the possibility of long-term institutional placement can bring about a complete breakdown of coping mechanisms, causing confusion. In such a situation, the provision of proper psychosocial counseling in dealing with the underlying stress may be beneficial in reversing the confusion. Likewise, allowing patients and residents to wander and providing a safe walking area may be all that is required to alleviate agitated behaviors.

During the period in which the underlying cause is being investigated, the patient or resident may continue to exhibit disturbed behaviors. To protect the individual from injuring him- or herself or others, it may be necessary to use a psychoactive drug in order to gain control over anxiety or aggression. In addition, if alternative approaches to eliminating the disturbed behavior are unsuccessful, psychoactive drugs may be required to improve the older individual's quality of life. Under such circumstances, obtaining a comprehensive drug history to guard against additive adverse effects and conducting laboratory studies to detect any hepatic or renal abnormalities that may influence the metabolism and excretion or elimination of the drug(s) must precede the use of psychoactive drugs. When a psychoactive is initiated, the prescriber should start with a low or small dose to test the person's responsiveness. Then the dosage should be increased slowly until the desired level of control is achieved without unwanted side effects. To ensure that psychoactive medications are used properly, staff should monitor patients and residents frequently for drug effectiveness and evidence of side effects. If drug therapy is unsuccessful or if the individual experiences adverse effects from the therapy, the medication should be discontinued and the plan of care revised. Also, staff must evaluate continually whether the person's disturbed behaviors have ceased or decreased in severity. In such an instance, staff should consider stopping the medication or reducing the dosage of the drug in order to avoid the risk of chemical restraint.

...

In summary, institutionally based health care providers play a major role in keeping patients and residents free of mechanical and chemical restraints. To meet this objective, providers should avoid the use of mechanical restraints to control falls and, instead, attempt restraint alternatives. With respect to chemical restraints, staff should limit exposure among older adults who have never used psychoactive medications to those with specific conditions. In addition, staff should reduce the dosage for individuals already using psychoactive drugs with the intent of stopping the drug, unless such a course is contraindicated clinically.

Notes

[1]Mechanical restraints are defined as any mechanical device, material, or equipment attached or adjacent to the individual's body that the person cannot remove easily and is used to inhibit free, independent movement. These devices include vest and chest jackets or harnesses, waist belts and sheets, leg ties, full-length bed side rails, wheelchair safety bars, and geri-chairs with fixed tray tables.

[2]All such rationale supporting the use of mechanical restraints are based on myth, not reality.

[3]Werner, P., Cohen-Mansfield, J., Braun, J., & Marx, M.S. (1989). Physical restraints and agitation in nursing home residents. *Journal of the American Geriatrics Society*, 37, 1122–1126.

[4]Tinetti, M.E., Liu, W.L., & Ginter, S.F. (1992). Mechanical restraint use and fall-related injury among residents of skilled nursing facilities. *Annals of Internal Medicine*, 116, 369–374.

Bibliography

An asterisk following a reference indicates a reference covering fall-risk assessment tools.

Hospital

Aisen, P.S., Deluca, T., & Lawlor, B.A. (1992). Falls among geropsychiatry inpatients are associated with PRN medications for agitation. *International Journal of Geriatric Psychiatry*, 7, 709–712.

Ashton, J., Gilbert, D., Hayward, G., et al. (1989). Predicting patient falls in an acute care setting. *Kansas Nurse*, 64(10), 3–5.

Baker, L. (1992). Developing a safety plan that works for patients and nurses. *Rehabilitation Nursing*, 17, 264–266.

Bates, D.W., Pruess, K., Souney, P., & Platt, R. (1995). Serious falls in hospitalized patients: Correlates and resource utilization. *American Journal of Medicine*, 99, 137–143.

Berryman, E., Gaskin, D., Jones, A., et al. (1989, July/August). Point by point: Predicting elders' falls. *Geriatric Nursing*, 199–201.*

Brady, R., Cheater, F.R., Pierce, L.L., et al. (1993). Geriatric falls: Prevention strategies for the staff. *Journal of Gerontological Nursing*, 19, 26–32.

Brians, L.K., Alexander, K., Grota, P., et al. (1991). The development of the RISK tool for fall prevention. *Rehabilitation Nursing*, 16(2), 67–69.*

Burden, B., & Kishi, D. (1989). Patient falls: Lowering the risk. *Nursing*, 16(2), 79.*

Byers, V., Arrington, M.E., & Finstuen, K. (1990). Predictive risk factors associated with stroke patient falls in acute care settings. *Journal of Neuroscience Nursing*, 22(3), 147–154.

Caley, L.M., & Pinchoff, D.M. (1994). A comparison study of patient falls in a psychiatric setting. *Hospital and Community Psychiatry*, 45, 823–825.

Cohen, L., & Guin, P. (1991). Implementation of a patient fall prevention program. *Journal of Neuroscience Nursing*, 23(5), 315–319.

Commodore, D.I. (1995) Falls in the elderly population: A look at incidence, risks, healthcare costs, and preventive strategies. *Rehabilitation Nursing*, 20(2), 84–89.

Corbett, C., & Pennypacker, B. (1992). Using a quality improvement team to reduce patient falls. *Journal of Hospital Quality*, 14, 38–54.*

Dallaire, L.B., & Burke, E.V. (1989). Reducing patient falls. *Nursing*, 19(1), 65.

Easterling, M.L. (1990). Which of your patients is headed for a fall? RN, 53(1), 56–59.

Gaebler, S. (1993). Predicting which patient will fall again . . . and again. *Journal of Advanced Nursing*, 18, 1895–1902.

Goodwin, M.B., & Westbrook, J.I. (1993). An analysis of patient accidents in hospital. *Australian Clinical Review*, 13, 141–149.

Hendrich, A.L. (1988). An effective unit based fall prevention plan. *Journal of Nursing Quality Assurance*, 3(1), 28–36.*

Hendrich, A.L. (1988). Unit based fall prevention. *Journal of Quality Assurance*, 10(1), 15–17.

Hill, B.A., Johnson, R., & Garrett, B.J. (1988). Reducing the incidence of falls in high-risk patients. *Journal of Nursing Administration*, 18(7/8), 24–28.*

Jones, W., & Smith, A. (1989). Preventing hospital incidence. What can we do? *Nursing Management*, 20(9), 58–60.

Kilpack, V., Boehm, J., Smith, N., & Mudge, B. (1991). Using research-based interventions to decrease patient falls. *Applied Nursing Research*, 4(2), 50–56.

Lawerence, J.I., & Maher, P.L. (1992). An interdisciplinary falls consult team: A collaborative approach to patient falls. *Journal of Nursing Care Quality*, 6(3), 21–29.

Llewellyn, J., Martin, B., Shekleton, M., & Firlit, S. (1988). Analysis of falls in the acute surgical and cardiovascular surgical patients. *Applied Nursing Research*, 1(3), 116–121.

Maciorowski, L.F., Munro, B.H., Dietrick-Gallagher, M., et al. (1988). A review of the patient fall literature. *Journal of Nursing Quality Assurance*, 3(1), 18–27.

Mayo, N.E., Korner-Bitensky, N., Becker, R., & Georges, P.C. (1989). Preventing falls among patients in a rehabilitation setting. *Canadian Journal of Rehabilitation*, 2(4), 235–240.

McCollam, M.E. (1995). Evaluation and implementation of a research-based falls assessment program. *Nursing Clinics of North America*, 30(3), 507–514.*

McFarlane, M.A., & Melora, P. (1993). Decreasing falls by the application of standards of care, practice, and governance. *Journal of Nursing Care Quality*, 8(1), 43–50.

Mion, L.C., Gregor, S., Buettner, M., et al. (1989). Falls in the rehabilitation setting: Incidence and characteristics. *Rehabilitation Nursing*, 14(1), 17–22.

Morse, J.M., Black, C., Oberle, K., & Donahue, P. (1989). A prospective study to identify the fall-prone patient. *Social Science Medicine*, 28(1), 81–86.*

Morse, J.M., Morse, R.M., & Tylko, S. (1989). Development of a scale to identify the fall-prone patient. *Canadian Journal on Aging*, 8, 366–377.*

Morton, D. (1989). Five years of fewer falls. *American Journal of Nursing*, 89(2), 204–205.

Quinlan, W.C. (1994). The liability risk of patients who fall. *Journal of Healthcare Risk Management*, 14, 29–33.

Roberts, B.L. (1993). Is stay in an intensive care unit a risk for falls? *Applied Nursing Research*, 6, 135–136.

Rohde, J.M., Myers, A.H., & Vlahov, D. (1990). Variation in risk for falls by clinical department: Implications for prevention. *Infection Control and Hospital Epidemiology*, 11, 521–524.

Ross, J.E.R. (1991). Iatrogenesis in the elderly: Contributors to falls. *Journal of Gerontological Nursing*, 17(9), 19–23.

Ruckstuhl, M.C., Marchionda, E.E., Salmons, J., & Larrabee, J.H. (1988). Patient falls: An outcome indicator. *Journal of Gerontological Nursing*, 6(1), 25–29.*

Schmid, N.A. (1990). Reducing patient falls: A research-based comprehensive fall prevention program. *Military Medicine*, 155, 202–207.

Spellbring, A.M. (1992). Assessing elderly patients at high risk for falls: A reliability study. *Journal of Nursing Care Quality*, 6(3), 30–35.*

Spellbring, A.M., Gannon, M.E., Kleckner, T., & Conway, K. (1988). Improving safety for hospitalized elderly. *Journal of Gerontological Nursing*, 14, 31–36.*

Tutuarima, J.A., de Haan, R.J., & Limburg, M. (1993). Number of nursing staff and falls: A case-control study by stroke patients in acute-care settings. *Journal of Advanced Nursing*, 18, 1101–1105.

Vlahov, D., Myers, A.H., & Al-Ibrahim, M.S. (1990). Epidemiology of falls among patients in a rehabilitation hospital. *Archives of Physical Medicine and Rehabilitation*, 71, 8–12.

Way, B.B. (1992). The relationship between staff–patient ratio and reported patient incidents. *Hospital and Community Psychiatry*, 43, 361–365.

Whedon, M.B., & Shedd, P. (1989). Prediction and prevention of patient falls. *Image: Journal of Nursing Scholarship*, 21(2), 108–114.*

Zepp, S. (1991). Ban "a" fall: A nursing innovation to reducing patient falls. *Kansas Nurse*, 66(7), 13.

NURSING FACILITY

Franzoni, S., Rozzini, R., Boffelli, S., et al. (1994). Fear of falling in nursing home residents. *Gerontology*, 40, 38–44.

Friedman, S.M., Williamson, J.D., Lee, B.H., et al. (1995). Increased fall rates in nursing home residents after relocation to a new facility. *Journal of the American Geriatrics Society*, 43, 1237–1242.

Ginter, S.G., & Mion, L.C. (1992). Falls in the nursing home: Preventable or inevitable? *Journal of Gerontological Nursing*, 18, 43–48.

Gross, Y.T., Shimamoto, Y., Rose, C.L., et al. (1990). Why do they fall? Monitoring risk factors in nursing homes. *Journal of Gerontological Nursing*, 16(6), 20–25.

Harris, P.B. (1989). Organizational and staff attitudinal determinants of falls in nursing home residents. *Medical Care*, 27, 737–749.

Janitti, P.O., Pyykko, I., & Laippala, P. (1995). Prognosis of falls among elderly nursing home residents. *Aging: Clinical and Experimental Research*, 7, 23–27.

Jonsson, P.V., Lipsitz, L.A., Kelley, M., et al. (1990). Hypotensive responses to common daily activities in institutional elderly: A potential risk for recurrent falls. *Archives of Internal Medicine*, 150, 1518–1524.

Kerman, M., & Mulvihill, M. (1990). The role of medication in falls among the elderly in a long-term care facility. *Mount Sinai Journal of Medicine*, 57, 343–347.

Kuehn, A.F., & Sendelweck, S. (1995). Acute health status and its relationship to falls in the nursing home. *Journal of Gerontological Nursing*, 21(7), 41–49.

Lipsitz, L.A., Jonsson, P.V., Kelley, M.M., et al. (1991). Causes and correlates of recurrent falls in ambulatory frail elderly. *Journal of Gerontology*, 46, M114–M122.

Luukinen, H., Koski, K., Laippala, P., & Kivela, S.L. (1995). Risk factors for recurrent falls in the elderly in long-term institutional care. *Public Health*, 109(1), 57–65.

Miceli, D.L.G., Wasman, H., Cavalieri, T., & Lage, S. (1994). Prodromal falls among older nursing home residents. *Applied Nursing Research*, 7(1), 18–27.

Myers, A.H., Baker, S.P., Robinson, E.G., et al. (1989). Falls in the institutionalized elderly. *Journal of Long-Term Care Administration*, 17(4), 12–16.

Myers, A.H., Baker, S.P., Van Natta, M.L., et al. (1991). Risk factors associated with falls and injuries among elderly institutionalized persons. *American Journal of Epidemiology*, 133, 1179–1190.

Myers, A.H., Van Natta, M.L., Robinson, E.G., & Baker, S.P. (1994). Can injurious falls be prevented? *Journal of Long-Term Care Administration*, 22(2), 26–29, 32.

Neufeld, R.R., Tideiksaar, R., Yew, E., et al. (1991). A multidisciplinary falls consultation service in a nursing home. *Gerontologist*, 31, 120–123.

Robbins, A.S., Rubenstein, L.Z., Josephson, K.R., et al. (1989). Predictors of falls among elderly people: Results of two population-based studies. *Archives of Internal Medicine*, 149, 1628–1633.*

Ross, J.E.R. (1991). Contributors to falls. *Journal of Gerontological Nursing*, 17, 19–23.

Rubenstein, L.Z., Josephson, K.R., & Osterweil, D. (1996). Falls and fall prevention in the nursing home. *Clinics of Geriatric Medicine*, 12(4), 881–902.

Rubenstein, L.Z., Josephson, K.R., & Robbins, A.S. (1994). Falls in the nursing home. *Annals of Internal Medicine*, 121, 442–451.

Rubenstein, L.Z., Robbins, A.S., Josephson, K.R., et al. (1990). The value of assessing falls in an elderly population. A randomized clinical trial. *Annals of Internal Medicine*, 113, 308–316.

Ruthazer, R., & Lipsitz, L.A. (1993). Antidepressants and falls among elderly people in long-term care. *American Journal of Public Health*, 83, 746–749.

Svensson, M.L., Rundgren, A., Larsson, M., et al. (1991). Accidents in the institutionalized elderly: A risk analysis. *Aging*, 3, 181–192.

Thappa, P.B., Brockman, K.G., Gideon, P., et al. (1996). Injurious falls in nonambulatory nursing home residents: A comparative study of circumstances, incidence, and risk factors. *Journal of the American Geriatrics Society*, 44, 273–278.

Thappa, P.B., Gideon, P., Brockman, K.G., et al. (1996). Clinical and biomechanical measures of balance as fall predictors in ambulatory nursing home residents. *Journal of Gerontology*, 51A, M239–M246.

Thappa, P.B., Gideon, P., Fought, R.L., & Ray, W.A. (1995). Psychotropic drugs and the risk of recurrent falls in ambulatory nursing home residents. *American Journal of Epidemiology*, 142, 202–211.

van Dijk, P.T.M., Meulenberg, O.G.R.M., van de Sande, H.J., & Habbema, J.D.F. (1993). Falls in demented patients. *Gerontologist*, 33, 200–204.

Wright, B.A., Aizenstein, S., Vogler, G., et al. (1990). Frequent fallers: Leading groups to identify psychological factors. *Journal of Gerontological Nursing*, 16(4), 15–19.

Young, S.W., Abedzadeh, C.B., & White, M.W. (1989). A fall-prevention program for nursing homes. *Nursing Management*, 20(11), 80Y, 80Z, 80AA, 80DD, 80FF.

Restraints

Blakeslee, J.A., Goldman, B.D., Papougenis, D., & Torell, C.A. (1991). Making the transition to restraint-free care. *Journal of Gerontological Nursing*, 17(2), 4–8.

Bradley, L., & Dufton, B. (1995). Breaking free. *Canadian Nurse*, 91(1), 36–40.

Bradley, L., Siddique, C.M., & Dufton, B. (1995). Reducing the use of physical restraints in long-term care facilities. *Journal of Gerontological Nursing*, 21(9), 21–34.

Brower, H.T. (1991). The alternative to restraints. *Journal of Gerontological Nursing*, 17, 18–22.

Brungardt, G.S. (1994). New guidelines for a less restrictive approach. *Geriatrics*, 49, 43–50.

Bruno, R. (1994). Policy for the people: One facility's introduction to restraint reduction. *Journal of Gerontological Social Work*, 22(3/4), 129–142.

Bryant, H., & Fernald, L. (1997). Nursing knowledge and use of restraint alternatives: Acute and chronic care. *Geriatric Nursing*, 18(2), 57–60.

Burton, L.C., German, P.S., Rovner, B.W., & Brandt, L.J. (1992). Physical restraint use and cognitive decline among nursing home residents. *Journal of the American Geriatrics Society*, 40, 811–816.

Calabrese, S., Paulic, T., Callicott, D., et al. (1992). Restraint review committee: A working model. *Perspectives*, 16, 2–6.

Capezuti, E., Evans, L., Strumpf, N., & Maislin, G. (1996). Physical restraint use and falls in nursing home residents. *Journal of the American Geriatrics Society*, 44, 627–633.

Chambers, J. (1993). Eliminating physical restraint use: Implications for practice. *Journal of Nursing Administration*, 23, 5.

Clavon, A.M. (1991). Implementation of a restraint policy: A case study. *Military Medicine*, 156, 499–501.

Conely, L., & Campbell, L. (1991). The use of restraints in caring for the elderly: Realities, consequences, and alternatives. *Nurse Practitioner*, 16(12), 48–52.

Cutchins, C.H. (1991). Blueprint for restraint-free care. *American Journal of Nursing*, 91(7), 36–42.

Dodds, S. (1996). Exercising restraint: Autonomy, welfare and elderly patients. *Journal of Medical Ethics*, 22(3), 160–163.

Dunbar, J.M., Neufeld, R.R., White, H.C., & Libow, L.S. (1996). Retrain, don't restrain: The educational intervention of the National Nursing Home Restraint Removal Project. *Gerontologist*, 36(4), 539–542.

Eigsti, D.G., & Vrooman, N. (1992). Releasing restraints in the nursing home: It can be done. *Journal of Gerontological Nursing*, 18(1), 21–23.

Ejaz, F.K., Flomar, S.J., Kaufmann, M., et al. (1994). Restraint reduction: Can it be achieved? *Gerontology*, 34, 694–699.

Ejaz, F.K., Jones, J.A., & Rose, M.S. (1994). Falls among nursing home residents: An examination of incident reports before and after restraint reduction programs. *Journal of the American Geriatrics Society*, 42, 960–964.

Evans, L.K., & Strumpf, N. (1989). Tying down the elderly: A review of the literature on physical restraints. *Journal of the American Geriatrics Society*, 36, 65–74.

Evans, L.K., & Strumpf, N. (1990). Myths about elder restraint. *Image: Journal of Nursing Scholarship*, 22, 124–128.

Evans, L.K., & Strumpf, N.E. (1992). Alternatives to physical restraints. *Journal of Gerontological Nursing*, 18, 5–11.

Evans, L.K., Strumpf, N.E., Allen-Taylor, S.L., et al. (1997). A clinical trial to reduce restraints in nursing homes. *Journal of the American Geriatrics Society*, 45, 675–681.

Fletcher, K.R. (1990). Restraints should be a last resort. RN, 53, 52–55.

Frank, C., Hodgetts, G., & Puxty, J. (1996). Safety and efficacy of physical restraint for the elderly. Review of the evidence. *Canadian Family Physician*, 42, 2402–2409.

Hall, M., & Marr, J. (1993). Patient restraint: A new philosophy. *Leadership in Health Services*, 2(4), 22–26, 42.

Hardin, S.B., Magee, R., Stratman, D., et al. (1994). Extended care and nursing home attitudes toward restraints. *Journal of Gerontological Nursing*, 20(3), 23–31.

Helmuth, A.M. (1995). Nurses' attitudes toward older persons on the use of physical restraints. *Orthopedic Nursing*, 14(2), 43–51.

Hennessy, C.H., Mcnelly, E.A., Whittington, F.J., et al. (1997). Perceptions of physical restraint use and barriers to restraint reduction in a long-term care facility. *Journal of Aging Studies*, 11(1), 49–62.

Janelli, L.M. (1995). Physical restraint use in acute care settings. *Journal of Nursing Care Quality*, 9(3), 86–92.

Janelli, L.M., Dickerson, S.S., & Ventura, M.R. (1995). Nursing staff's experiences using restraints. *Clinical Nursing Research*, 4(4), 425–441.

Janelli, L.M., Kanski, G.W., & Neary, M.A. (1994). Physical restraints: Has OBRA made a difference? *Journal of Gerontological Nursing*, 20, 17–21.

Janelli, L.M., Scherer, Y.K., Kanski, G.W., & Neary, M.A. (1991). What nursing staff members really know about physical restraints. *Rehabilitation Nursing*, 16, 345–349.

Janelli, L.M., Scherer, Y.K., Kuhn, M.M., et al. (1994). Acute/critical care nurses' knowledge of physical restraints. *Journal of Nursing Staff Development*, 10, 6–11.

Johnson, S.H. (1990). The fear of liability and the use of restraints in nursing homes. *Law, Medicine and Health Care*, 18, 263–273.

Johnson, S.H. (1991). Nursing home restraints: The legal issues. *Health Progress*, 23, 18–19.

Kallmann, S.L. (1992). Comfort, safety, and independence: Restraint release and its challenges. *Geriatric Nursing*, 13(3), 143–148.

Kane, R.L., Williams, C.C., Williams, T.F., et al. (1993). Restraining restraints: Changes in a standard of care. *Annual Review of Public Health*, 14, 545–584.

Kapp, M.B. (1992). Nursing home restraints and legal liability. *Journal of Legal Medicine*, 13, 1–32.

Leger-Krall, S. (1994). When restraints become abusive. *Nurse*, 24, 55–56.

Levine, J.M., Marchello, V., & Totolos, E. (1995). Progress toward a restraint-free environment in a large academic nursing facility. *Journal of the American Geriatrics Society*, 43, 914–918.

Lofgren, R.P., MacPherson, D.S., Granieri, R., et al. (1989). Mechanical restraints on the medical wards: Are protective devices safe? *American Journal of Public Health*, 79, 735–738.

MacPherson, D.S., Lofgren, R.P., Granier, R., et al. (1990). Deciding to restrain medical patients. *Journal of the American Geriatrics Society*, 38, 516–520.

Magee, R., Hyatt, E.C., Hardin, S.B., et al. (1993). Institutional policy: Use of restraints in extended care and nursing homes. *Journal of Gerontological Nursing*, 19(4), 31–39.

Martin, L.S., & Huges, S.R. (1993). Using the mission statement to craft a least-restraint policy. *Nursing Management*, 24(3), 65–66.

Master, R., & Marks, S.F. (1990). The use of restraints. *Rehabilitation Nursing*, 15, 22–25.

Mercurio, A.T., & Mion, L.C. (1992). Methods to reduce restraints: Process, outcomes, and future directions. *Journal of Gerontological Nursing*, 18, 5–11.

Miles, S.H., & Irvine, P. (1992). Deaths caused by physical restraint. *Gerontologist*, 32, 762–766.

Mion, L.C., Frengley, J.D., Jakovicic, C.A., et al. (1989). A further exploration of the use of physical restraints in hospitalized patients. *Journal of the American Geriatrics Society*, 37, 949–956.

Mion, L.C., Strump, N., & Fulmer, T. (1994). Use of physical restraints in the hospital setting: Implications for the nurse. *Geriatric Nursing*, 15(3), 127–134.

Morse, J.M., & McHutchion, E. (1991). The behavioral effects of releasing restraints. *Research in Nursing and Health*, 14, 187–196.

Neufeld, R.R., Libow, L.S., Foley, W., & White, H. (1995). Can physically restrained nursing-home residents be untied safely? Intervention and evaluation design. *Journal of the American Geriatrics Society*, 43, 1264–1268.

Newbern, V.B., & Lindsey, I.H. (1994). Attitudes of wives toward having their elderly husbands restrained. *Geriatric Nursing*, 15, 135–138.

Patterson, J.E., Stumpf, N.E., & Evans, L.K. (1995). Nursing consultation to reduce restraints in a nursing home. *Clinical Nurse Specialist*, 9(4), 231–235.

Phillips, C., Hawes, C., & Fries, B. (1993). Reducing the use of restraints in nursing homes: Will it increase costs? *American Journal of Public Health*, 83(3), 342–348.

Quinn, C.A. (1993). Nurses' perceptions about physical restraints. *Western Journal of Nursing Research*, 15, 148–162.

Rader, J. (1991). Modifying the environment to decrease the use of restraints. *Journal of Gerontological Nursing*, 17, 9–13.

Rader, J., Semradek, J., McKenzie, D., & McMahon, M. (1992). Restraint strategies: Reducing restraints in Oregon's long-term care facilities. *Journal of Gerontological Nursing*, 18(11), 49–56.

Registered Nurses' Association of Nova Scotia. (1995). Position statement on the use of physical restraints. . . approved by the RNANS Board of Directors, April 12, 1995. *Nurse to Nurse*, 6(3), 19.

Rodgers, S. (1994). Reducing restraints in a rehabilitation setting: A safer environment through team effort. *Rehabilitation Nursing*, 19, 274–276.

Scherer, Y.K., Janelli, L.M., Wu, Y.B., & Kuhn, M.M. (1993). Restrained patients: An important issue for critical care nursing. *Heart and Lung*, 22, 77–83.

Schirm, V., Gray, M., & Peoples, M. (1993). Nursing personnel's perceptions of physical restraint in long-term care. *Clinical Nursing Research*, 2, 98–110.

Schnelle, J.F., MacRae, P.G., Simmons, S.F., et al. (1994). Safety assessment for the frail elderly: A comparison of restrained and unrestrained nursing home residents. *Journal of the American Geriatrics Society*, 42, 586–592.

Schnelle, J.F., Newman, D.R., White, M., et al. (1992). Reducing and managing restraints in long term facilities. *Journal of the American Geriatrics Society*, 40, 381–385.

Shugrue, D.T., & Larocque, K.L. (1996). Reducing restraint use in the acute care setting. *Nursing Management*, 27(10), 32H, 32J, 32L, 32O.

Simmons, S.A., Schnelle, J.F., MacRaie, P.G., et al. (1995). Wheelchairs as mobility restraints: Predictors of wheelchair activity in nonambulatory nursing home residents. *Journal of the American Geriatrics Society*, 43, 384–388.

Sloane, P.D., Papougenis, D., & Blakeslee, J.A. (1992). Alternatives to physical and pharmacologic restraints in long-term care. *American Family Physician*, 45, 763–769.

Stolley, J.M. (1995). Freeing your patients from restraints. *American Journal of Nursing*, 95(2), 26–31.

Stolley, S.M., King, J., Clarke, M., et al. (1993). Developing a restraint use policy for acute care. *Journal of Nursing Administration*, 23, 49–54.

Strumpf, N.E., Evans, L.K., Wagner, J., et al. (1992). Reducing physical restraints: Developing an educational program. *Journal of Gerontological Nursing*, 18, 21–27.

Sullivan-Marx, E.M. (1994). Delirium and physical restraints in hospitalized elderly. *Image: Journal of Nursing Scholarship*, 26, 295–300.

Sullivan-Marx, E.M. (1995). Psychological responses to physical restraint use in older adults. *Psychosocial Nursing*, 33(6), 20–25.

Sullivan-Marx, E.M. (1996). Restraint-free care: How does a nurse decide? *Journal of Gerontological Nursing*, 22(9), 7–14.

Sundel, M., Garrett, R.M., & Horn, R.D. (1994). Restraint reduction in a nursing home and its impact on employee attitudes. *Journal of the American Geriatrics Society*, 42, 381–387.

Thomas, A., Redfern, L., & John R. (1995). Perceptions of acute care nurses in the use of restraints. *Journal of Gerontological Nursing*, 21(6), 32–38.

Tinetti, M.E., Liu, W., & Ginter, S.F. (1992). Mechanical restraint use and fall-related injuries among residents of skilled nursing homes. *Annals of Internal Medicine*, 116, 369–374.

Tinetti, M.E., Liu, W., Marottolil, R.A., et al. (1991). Mechanical restraint use among skilled nursing facilities: Prevalence, patterns and predictors. *Journal of the American Medical Association*, 265, 460–471.

Wells, C.F., Brown, D., & McClymount, A.A. (1994). Development of a least restraint program—one hospital's experience. *Perspectives*, 18, 10–13.

Werner, P., Cohen-Mansfield, J., Braun, J., et al. (1989). Physical restraint and agitation in nursing home residents. *Journal of the American Geriatrics Society*, 37, 1122–1126.

Werner, P., Cohen-Mansfield, J., Koroknay, V., & Braun, J. (1994). Reducing restraint: Impact on staff attitudes. *Journal of Gerontological Nursing*, 20(12), 19–24.

Werner, P., Koroknay, V., Braun, J., & Cohen-Mansfield, J. (1994). Individualized care alternatives used in the process of removing physical restraints in the nursing home. *Journal of the American Geriatrics Society*, 42, 321–325.

Wilson, E.B. (1996). Physical restraint of elderly patients in critical care: Historical perspectives and new directions. *Critical Care Nursing Clinics of North America*, 8(1), 61–70.

appendix a

Performance-Oriented Environmental Mobility Screen (POEMS)

Instructions: Ask the patient or resident to perform the indicated maneuvers. If the individual uses an ambulation device (e.g., cane, walker), each maneuver is tested with the device as appropriate. For each maneuver, indicate whether the person's performance is normal (independent function) or impaired (dependent function). For each impairment discovered, suggested interventions (indicated by numbers in parentheses) to reduce fall risk are indicated. The key for the numbered interventions follows the forms.

Note: Each of the POEMS maneuvers has been printed on a separate page. The purpose of this design is to allow staff members to copy the POEMS and arrange the sequence of maneuvers according to their individual needs and those of patients or residents. In addition, the design allows for targeted assessments of risk (e.g., bed transfers, toilet transfers).

Ambulation

	Observation	
Bedroom	Normal	Impaired (Intervention)
Walk in straight line from doorway to most distant wall (approx. 10–15 feet)	❑ Gait is continuous, without hesitation	❑ Gait is noncontinuous, with hesitation (1) (2)
	❑ Gait is straight, without deviation from path	❑ Gait deviates from straight path (1) (2) (5)
	❑ Both feet clear floor surface	❑ One or both feet scrape floor surface (1) (5) (6)
	❑ Does not use walls / furniture for support	❑ Walls / furniture are used for support (1) (2) (3) (4)
		❑ Unable to perform maneuver or perform it safely (10)
Turn around, walk around both sides of bed	❑ Steps are smooth, continuous	❑ Steps are discontinuous (1) (2) (5)
	❑ Does not stagger or lose balance	❑ Staggers, loses balance (1) (2) (5)
	❑ Does not use walls / furniture for support	❑ Walls / furniture are used for support (1) (2) (3) (4)
		❑ Unable to perform maneuver or perform it safely (10)

(*continued*)

Ambulation (*continued*)

Bedroom	Normal	Impaired (Intervention)
Device used to perform maneuver: ❑ Yes Type ________ ❑ No	❑ Device appropriate for space	❑ Device inappropriate for space (2) (3)
	❑ Device used correctly	❑ Device used incorrectly (2)

Ambulation

	Observation	
Bathroom	Normal	Impaired (Intervention)
Walk to sink, toilet, turn around and return	❑ Gait is continuous, smooth without hesitation	❑ Gait is noncontinuous, with hesitation (1) (2)
	❑ Both feet clear floor and threshold	❑ One or both feet scrape floor or threshold (5) (6)
	❑ Does not lose balance	❑ Loses balance (1) (2)
	❑ Does not use walls, sink towel bar for balance support	❑ Uses walls, sink, towel bar for balance support (3) (4)
		❑ Unable to perform maneuver or perform it safely (10)
Device used to perform maneuver: ❑ Yes Type ________	❑ Device appropriate for space	❑ Device inappropriate for space (3)
❑ No	❑ Device used correctly	❑ Device used incorrectly (2)

Ambulation

	Observation	
Hallway	Normal	Impaired (Intervention)
Walk from bedroom to nurses' station, toward exit, and return to bedroom	❑ Gait is continuous, without hesitation	❑ Gait is noncontinuous, with hesitation (1) (2) (5)
	❑ Gait is straight, without deviation from path	❑ Gait deviates from straight path (1) (2) (5)
	❑ Both feet clear floor surface	❑ One or both feet scrape floor surface (1) (5) (6)
	❑ Does not use walls / furniture / handrails for support	❑ Walls / furniture / handrails are used for support (1) (2) (3) (4)
	❑ Able to perform maneuver without excessive fatigue	❑ Unable to perform maneuver without fatigue (1) (10)
		❑ Unable to perform maneuver or perform it safely (10)
Device used to perform maneuver: ❑ Yes Type ______ ❑ No	❑ Device appropriate for space	❑ Device inappropriate for space (3)
	❑ Device used correctly	❑ Device used incorrectly (2)

Transfers

Bed	Observation: Normal	Observation: Impaired (Intervention)
Transfer onto bed and lie down	❑ Bed transfer is completed in smooth, controlled movement (sits on bed in one attempt)	❑ Bed transfer is not smooth (requires several attempts; falls onto mattress; uses mattress edge to guide transfer) (1) (8)
	❑ Sitting balance is stable	❑ Sitting balance is unstable (2) (8)
	❑ Does not use arm support to maintain sitting balance	❑ Uses arm support to maintain sitting balance (2) (8)
	❑ Both feet rest flat on floor	❑ Feet do not rest flat on floor (8)
	❑ Feet do not slide	❑ Feet slide away (5) (6)
	❑ Bed does not slide away	❑ Bed slides away (6) (8)
	❑ Able to lie down in one smooth, controlled movement	❑ Unable to lie down in one smooth, controlled movement (several attempts required) (8)
		❑ Unable to perform maneuver or perform it safely (8) (10)
Device used to perform maneuver: ❑ Yes Type ________ ❑ No	❑ Device appropriate for space	❑ Device inappropriate for space (3)
	❑ Device used correctly	❑ Device used incorrectly (2)

(continued)

Transfers (*continued*)

Bed	Normal	Impaired (Intervention)
Rise from supine position and transfer off bed	❑ Able to rise in one smooth, controlled movement to sitting position	❑ Unable to rise in one smooth, controlled movement (several attempts required to assume sitting position or cannot perform) (1) (8)
	❑ Sitting balance is stable	❑ Sitting balance is unstable (2) (8)
	❑ Does not use arm support to maintain sitting balance	❑ Uses arm support to maintain sitting balance (2) (8)
	❑ Both feet rest flat on floor	❑ Feet do not rest flat on floor (8)
	❑ Transfers off bed in smooth, controlled movement (rises off bed in one attempt)	❑ Transfer off bed is not completed in smooth, controlled movement (requires several attempts) (8)
	❑ Feet do not slide	❑ Feet slide away (5) (6)
	❑ Bed does not slide away	❑ Bed slides away (6) (8)
		❑ Unable to perform maneuver or perform it safely (8) (10)

Transfers

	Observation	
Chair	Normal	Impaired (Intervention)
Sit down in chair(s)	❑ Sits in smooth, controlled movement (sits in one attempt)	❑ Sitting is not completed in smooth, controlled movement (requires several attempts) (1) (7)
	❑ Does not lose balance	❑ Loses balance (falls into seat) (2) (7)
	❑ Does not use arm rests for sitting	❑ Uses arm rests for sitting (7)
	❑ Chair does not tip or slide away	❑ Chair tips or slides away (7)
	❑ Seated, both feet rest flat on floor	❑ Seated, feet do not rest on floor (7)
		❑ Unable to perform maneuver or perform it safely (10)
Device used to perform maneuver: ❑ Yes Type ______	❑ Device appropriate for space	❑ Device inappropriate for space (2)
❑ No	❑ Device used correctly	❑ Device used incorrectly (2)

(continued)

Transfers (*continued*)

Chair	Normal	Impaired (Intervention)
Rises from chair	❑ Rises in smooth, controlled movement (rises in one attempt).	❑ Rising is not completed in smooth, controlled movement (requires several attempts) (1) (7)
	❑ Does not lose balance	❑ Loses balance (falls back into/off seat) (1) (7)
	❑ Does not use armrests	❑ Uses armrests or seat (7)
	❑ Chair does not tip or slide away	❑ Chair tips or slides away (7)
	❑ Feet do not slide on floor	❑ Feet slide on floor (5) (6) (7)
		❑ Unable to perform maneuver or perform it safely (10)

Transfers

	Observation	
Toilet	Normal	Impaired (Intervention)
Sit down on toilet	❑ Able to sit down in one smooth, controlled movement	❑ Unable to sit down in one smooth, controlled movement (requires several attempts) (1) (9)
	❑ Does not lose balance	❑ Loses balance (1) (2) (9)
	❑ Does not use grab bars, sink edge for balance support	❑ Uses grab bars, sink edge for balance support (3) (4) (9)
	❑ Both feet rest flat on floor in seated position	❑ Feet do not rest flat on floor in seated position (9)
		❑ Unable to perform maneuver or perform it safely (9) (10)
Device used to perform maneuver: ❑ Yes Type ________ ❑ No	❑ Device appropriate for space	❑ Device inappropriate for space (3)
	❑ Device used correctly	❑ Device used incorrectly (2)

(*continued*)

Transfers (*continued*)

Toilet	Normal	Impaired (Intervention)
Reach for toilet paper receptacle; simulate toilet hygiene	❑ Able to perform without excessive reach or balance loss	❑ Unable to perform without excessive reach or balance loss (9)
	❑ Does not use toilet, walls for balance support	❑ Uses toilet, walls for balance support (3) (9)
		❑ Unable to perform maneuver, or perform safely (10)
Rise from toilet	❑ Able to rise in one smooth, controlled movement	❑ Unable to rise in one smooth, controlled movement (requires several attempts) (1) (9)
	❑ Does not lose balance	❑ Loses balance (1) (3) (9)
	❑ Does not use grab bars, sink edge for balance support	❑ Uses grab bars, sink edge for balance support (3) (4) (9)
	❑ Feet do not slide away	❑ One or both feet slide away (5) (6)
		❑ Unable to perform maneuver or perform it safely (10)

Balance

Standing/Reaching	Observation: Normal	Impaired (Intervention)
Stand in place (for approx. 15 seconds) with both eyes open	❑ Steady, able to stand without losing balance	❑ Unsteady, unable to maintain standing balance (1) (2)
	❑ Does not use chair to maintain balance	❑ Uses chair to maintain balance (7)
	❑ Does not use device to maintain balance	❑ Uses device to maintain balance (1) (2)
		❑ Unable to perform maneuver or perform it safely (10)
Stand in place with both eyes closed	❑ Steady, able to stand without losing balance	❑ Unsteady, unable to maintain standing balance (1) (2) (4)
	❑ Does not use chair to maintain balance	❑ Uses chair to maintain balance (7)
Stand in place (both eyes open); lightly nudge person's sternum 3 times	❑ Steady, able to maintain balance	❑ Unsteady, unable to maintain balance (1) (2)
	❑ Does not use furniture or walls to maintain balance	❑ Uses furniture or walls to maintain balance (7)
		❑ Unable to perform maneuver or perform it safely (10)

(*continued*)

Balance (*continued*)

Standing / Reaching	Normal	Impaired (Intervention)
Bend down and pick up object from floor	❑ Steady, able to bend down without losing balance	❑ Unsteady, unable to bend down and maintain balance (1)
	❑ Does not use furniture to maintain balance	❑ Uses furniture to maintain balance (3)
	❑ Does not use device to maintain balance	❑ Unable to perform maneuver or perform it safely (10)

Key to Interventions

1. Medical evaluation
2. Rehabilitative evaluation
   - ❑ Device assessment
   - ❑ Gait assessment
   - ❑ Balance assessment
   - ❑ Exercise program
   - ❑ Hip-padding system
   - ❑ Other: ____________
3. Walking space/pathways
   - ❑ Unobstructed walking areas
   - ❑ Stable furnishing for balance support
   - ❑ Nonslip grasp surfaces (furnishings, walls, sink, hallways)
   - ❑ Other: ____________
4. Visual walking space/pathways
   - ❑ Accessible lighting
   - ❑ Adequate lighting
   - ❑ Glare reduction
   - ❑ Color contrast (furnishings, handrails, grab bars)
   - ❑ Other: ____________
5. Footwear
   - ❑ Podiatrist evaluation
   - ❑ Proper fit
   - ❑ Nonslip soles/socks
   - ❑ Nontraction soles
   - ❑ Other: ____________
6. Floor space
   - ❑ Nonslip finishes
   - ❑ Nonslip strips
   - ❑ Eliminate uneven surface elevations
   - ❑ Color contrast uneven surface elevations
   - ❑ Other: ____________
7. Chair
   - ❑ Seat height adjustment
   - ❑ Seat depth adjustment
   - ❑ Supportive armrests
   - ❑ Stable (nonmovable) chair
   - ❑ Seat cushions/wedge cushion
   - ❑ Other: ____________
8. Bed
   - ❑ Height adjustment (low/high)
   - ❑ Firm mattress support
   - ❑ Half bed side rail
   - ❑ Transfer bar
   - ❑ Bed wheel locks
   - ❑ Immobilizer legs
   - ❑ Bed alarm device
   - ❑ Accessible nurse call system
   - ❑ Other: ____________
9. Toilet
   - ❑ Grab bar (wall/toilet attached)
   - ❑ Raised toilet seat
   - ❑ Accessible nurse call system
   - ❑ Bedside commode
   - ❑ Other: ____________
10. Human assistance
    - ❑ One person
    - ❑ Two people
    - ❑ Other: ____________

POEMS Summary

Location	Maneuver	Normal	Impaired
Bedroom	Ambulation		
	Straight line	❑	❑
	Turning	❑	❑
	Chair transfer		
	Onto	❑	❑
	Off	❑	❑
	Standing balance		
	Eyes open	❑	❑
	Eyes closed	❑	❑
	Sternal nudge	❑	❑
	Bending down	❑	❑
	Bed transfer		
	Onto	❑	❑
	Off	❑	❑
Bathroom	Ambulation		
	Straight line	❑	❑
	Turning	❑	❑
	Toilet transfer		
	Onto	❑	❑
	Off	❑	❑
	Toilet hygiene	❑	❑
Hallway	Ambulation		
	Straight line	❑	❑
	Turning	❑	❑
	Distance	❑	❑

appendix b

Ambulation Device Measurement

Cane Measurements

The measurement of cane height is the same regardless of cane type. Ask the person wearing everyday shoes to stand erect, with arms hanging loosely by his or her sides. The cane (or center of a multistem cane) is placed approximately 6 inches to the front and side of the person's shoe.

Two landmarks are used to determine proper height, the greater trochanter and the angle of the elbow. The top of the cane should come to approximately the level of the greater trochanter and the elbow should be flexed at 20°–30°. The degree of elbow flexion is the most important indicator of correct height because it allows the arm to shorten or lengthen during different phases of gait. This degree of flex-

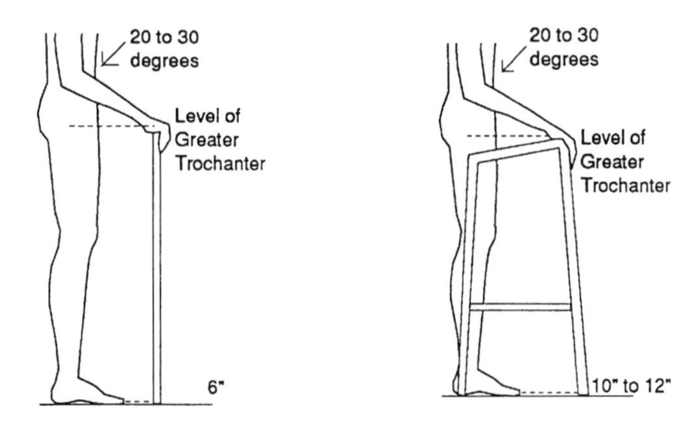

ion prevents the person from leaning forward or into the cane (if too short) or away, leaning precariously backward (if too tall).

Walker Measurements

The measurement of walker height is similar to that of a cane. Place the walker 10–12 inches in front of the feet so that the walker partially surrounds the person. In this position, the handles should come to approximately the greater trochanter and the elbow is flexed at 20°–30°.

appendix c

Ambulation Device Utilization

Cane Ambulation: Level Ground

For cane ambulation on level ground, the cane is held on the side of the body that is opposite to the affected limb. This position provides the greatest base of support and simulates normal gait. When the cane is held on the same side of the body as that of the affected limb, the person's center of gravity shifts from side to side. This position produces an abnormal, uncomfortable gait and leads to instability.

The cane and the involved extremity are advanced simultaneously (see figure at top of p. 168). The cane is held relatively close to the body and should not be placed ahead of the affected limb. Placing the cane too far to the side or forward will cause lateral bending, forward bending, or both, resulting in a loss of stability.

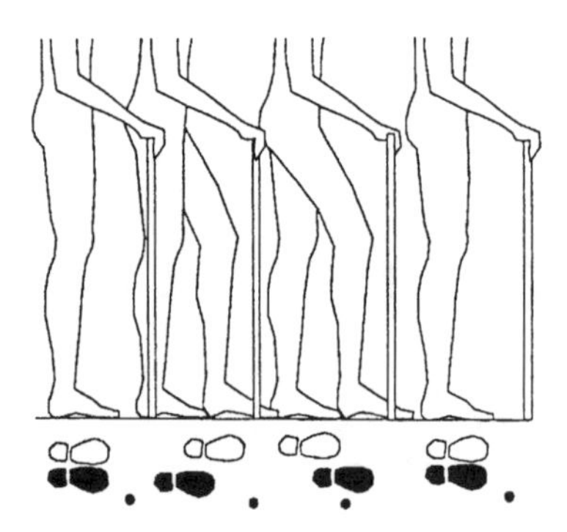

Walker Ambulation: Level Ground

Standard Walker

Ambulation using the standard walker on level ground requires the person to have enough stability to balance on one or both feet while he or she picks up the walker and moves it forward. The "step to" and "step through" gaits are the gaits used most often for stability and to protect arthritic joints. Weight is placed on hands (i.e., push down on walker) and, at the same time, the other, unaffected foot is moved forward, either parallel to ("step to" gait) or past ("step through" gait) the opposite, affected foot. The person should not step too close to the front bar of the walker because this motion decreases the base of support and may cause the person to fall backward.

Sliding Walker

The use of the sliding walker is similar to that of the standard walker, except that the walker is not picked up but slid along the floor. A "step to" or "step through" gait is employed.

Rolling Walker

Weight is shifted from all four walker legs to the forward (wheeled) legs. The walker is rolled forward until the hands are 10–12 inches ahead of the feet. A "step to" or "step through" gait is employed.

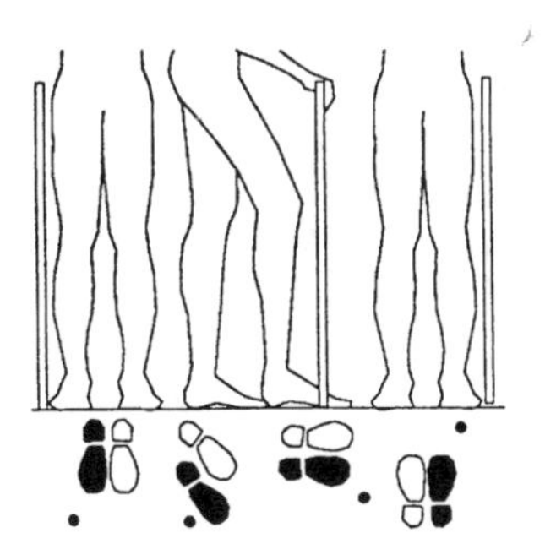

Cane Ambulation: Turning

Turning is accomplished by moving to the unaffected side using a gait similar to that used when walking on level ground surfaces. To start, feet are kept slightly spread apart in order to maintain balance. The cane and feet are moved in a small circle. The following sequence is used: First, the cane and the affected limb are moved, then the unaffected limb is moved. The unaffected limb is kept on the inside of the circle. The person should not pivot on the unaffected limb to maintain his or her balance. The process is repeated until the turn is complete.

Walker Ambulation: Turning

Turning with a walker is similar to that of turning with a cane. A "step to" or "step through" gait is employed.

Cane Transfers: Standing

In making a cane transfer to the standing position (see figure at top of p. 170), the person slides forward to the edge of his or her seat. The standard cane is placed against the chair armrest; the quad cane or hemiwalker cane is positioned in front and to the unaffected side of the body. The person places the feet in the stride position (i.e., unaffected leg behind affected leg) with both hands on the armrests, leans forward and comes to a standing position, and then grasps cane.

Walker Transfers: Standing

In making a walker transfer to the standing position, the person moves forward to the edge of his or her seat. The walker is positioned directly

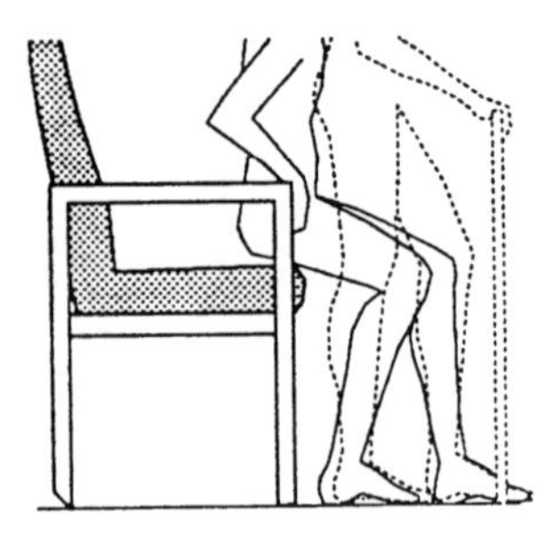

in front of the chair. The person places the feet in the stride position (i.e., unaffected leg behind affected leg), grasps both armrests of the chair, leans forward and comes to a standing position by pushing down on the armrests, and then reaches for the walker.

Cane Transfers: Sitting

In making a cane transfer to the sitting position, the person approaches the chair, turns in a small circle toward the unaffected side of the body, and backs up until the chair edge is felt against the legs. The person reaches for the chair armrest with his or her free hand, releases the broad-based cane or leans the standard cane against the chair, grasps the opposite armrest, and sits down.

Walker Transfers: Sitting

In making a walker transfer to the sitting position, the person approaches the chair, turns in a small circle toward the unaffected side of the body, and backs up until the chair edge is felt against the legs. The person reaches for one chair armrest at a time, releases his or her grasp on the walker, and sits down.

appendix d

Preventing Falls and Fractures

An injury from falling can limit a person's ability to lead an active, independent life. This is especially true for older people. Each year thousands of older men and women are injured, sometimes permanently, by falls that result in broken bones. Yet many of these injuries can be prevented by making simple changes in the home.

As people age, changes in their vision, hearing, muscle strength, coordination, and reflexes may make them susceptible to falls. Older adults likely have treatable disorders that may affect their balance (e.g., diabetes; conditions of the heart, nervous system, and thyroid). In addition, as compared with younger adults, older people often take medications that may cause dizziness or lightheadedness.

Preventing falls is especially important for people with osteoporosis, a condition in which bone mass decreases so that bones are more fragile and break easily. Osteoporosis is a major cause of bone fractures in women after menopause and older adults in general. For people with severe osteoporosis, even a minor fall may cause one or more bones to break.

Steps to Take

Falls and accidents seldom "just happen," and many can be prevented. Each of us can take steps to make our homes safer and reduce the likelihood of falling. Here are some guidelines to help prevent falls and fractures:

- Vision and hearing should be tested regularly and properly corrected.
- The patient or resident should talk with the doctor or pharmacist about the side effects of the medicines he or she is taking and whether they affect coordination or balance. The person should ask for suggestions to reduce the possibility of falling.
- The person should limit his or her alcohol intake. Even a small amount of alcohol can disturb already-impaired balance and reflexes.
- The patient or resident should use caution in getting up too quickly after eating, lying down, or resting. Low blood pressure may cause dizziness at these times.
- The nighttime temperature in the person's home should be at least 65°F. Prolonged exposure to cold temperatures may cause a drop in body temperature, which in turn may lead to dizziness and falling. Many older adults cannot tolerate cold as well as younger people can.
- A cane, walking stick, or walker should be used to help the person maintain balance on uneven or unfamiliar ground or if the person sometimes feels dizzy. Special caution should be taken in walking outdoors on wet or icy pavement.
- The patient or resident should wear supportive rubber-soled or low-heeled shoes and avoid wearing smooth-soled slippers or only socks on stairs and waxed floors. These surfaces make it easy to slip.
- The person should maintain a regular program of exercise to improve strength and muscle tone, and joints, tendons, and

ligaments should be kept flexible. Many older people enjoy walking and swimming. Mild weight-bearing activities, such as walking or climbing stairs, may even reduce bone loss due to osteoporosis. The person should check with his or her doctor or physical therapist to plan a suitable exercise program.

Make Home a Safe Place

Many older people fall because of hazardous conditions at home. This checklist can be used to help safeguard the person against some likely hazards.

Stairways, hallways, and pathways should have

- Good lighting; provide extra lighting along path from bedroom to bathroom, by one- and two-step elevations, and by top and bottom of stairway landings; use night-lights, 100- to 200-watt bulbs, and 3-way lightbulbs to increase lighting levels
- A lack of glare—Eliminate glare from exposed lightbulbs by using translucent light shades or frosted lightbulbs
- Firmly attached carpet, rough texture or abrasive strips to secure footing; nonskid rugs and carpet runners on slippery floors; a coating of nonskid floor wax; carpeting over threshold to create a smooth transition between rooms
- No clutter, including obtrusive furnishings
- Tightly fastened cylindrical handrails running the whole length and along both sides of all stairs, with light switches at the top and bottom

Bathrooms should have

- Elevated toilet seat or toilet safety frame
- Wall-mounted or tub-attached grab bar or shower chair/tub transfer bench
- Nonskid mats, abrasive strips, or carpet on all surfaces that may get wet
- Night-lights

Bedrooms should have

- Night-lights or light switches within reach of bed(s)
- Telephones that are easy to reach near the bed(s)

Living areas should have

- Electrical cords and telephone wires placed away from walking paths
- Rugs well secured to the floor
- Furniture, especially low coffee tables, and other objects arranged so that they are not obstacles
- Couches and chairs that are of a proper height so that patients or residents get into and out of them easily (add a seat cushion to raise seat height; replace existing mattress with one that is thinner, to lower bed height, or thicker, to raise bed height); chairs with armrest support
- Frequently used objects sited at waist level
- A reacher device available for person to obtain objects from shelves
- Shelves and cupboards at accessible height

Some material adapted from *National Institutes of Health Age Page: Preventing Falls and Fractures*, 1992.

appendix e

Case Studies

CASE 1*

E.L. *is an 80-year-old hospital patient who experienced two falls. She stated that both falls occurred shortly after she got up from bed at night to go to the bathroom. She was hurrying to the toilet in order to avoid urinating on the floor and lost her balance. Her medical problems consist of* Parkinson's *disease and arthritis in both knees. She takes no medication.* E.L.'s *ambulation is poor and she does not use a walker. Her cognitive abilities are unaffected.*

Questions

1. With the information you have about this patient, what specific interventions would you include in her care plan in order to reduce fall risk?

*Answers to the individual case questions begin on page 179.

2. Based on your care plan, for which outcomes would you monitor this patient?

Case 2

G.B. is a 76-year-old nursing facility resident who experienced several falls from bed. He complained of unsteadiness after getting up from bed. G.B.'s medical problems include a history of hypertension, which was treated with a diuretic. The results of the medical evaluation revealed that G.B. was dehydrated and had orthostatic hypotension (i.e., dizziness on rising from a seated or lying position).

Questions

1. With the information you have about this resident, what specific interventions would you include in his care plan in order to reduce fall risk?
2. Based on your care plan, for which outcomes would you monitor this resident?

Case 3

M.P. is an 89-year-old nursing facility resident who experienced several falls, all of which occurred while she was walking either in the bedroom or hallway in the late afternoon. M.P.'s medical problems consist of severe dementia. She exhibits poor gait and balance. M.P. has a walker, but forgets to use it. Since her original diagnosis, M.P.'s cognition has deteriorated further, resulting in agitation. M.P. does not take medication.

Questions

1. With the information you have about this resident, what specific interventions would you include in her care plan in order to reduce fall risk?
2. Based on your care plan, for which outcomes would you monitor this resident?

Case 4

J.S. is an 82-year-old hospital patient who was admitted for pneumonia. He remained in bed for 3 days. After treatment of the infection, the patient demonstrated poor bed and toilet transfers, which was the result of lower-leg weakness developed after being confined to bed.

Questions

1. With the information you have about this patient, what specific interventions would you include in his care plan in order to improve mobility and reduce fall risk?
2. Based on your care plan, for which outcomes would you monitor this patient?

Case 5

L.R. *is a 73-year-old hospital patient admitted for falls. After her most recent fall, she lay on the floor unattended for* 6 *hours (she lives alone).* L.R.*'s falls are associated with a loss of balance—when she reaches up to retrieve objects from her kitchen and closet shelves and when she gets into and out of her bathtub.* L.R. *has experienced a stroke and, as a result, has mild left-side leg weakness. She expresses a fear of falling.*

Questions

1. With the information you have about this patient, what specific interventions would you include in her care plan in order to improve mobility and reduce her fear of falls while she is in the hospital?
2. What specific interventions would you include in her post-discharge care plan?

Case 6

A.C. *is a* 91*-year-old nursing facility resident who has experienced several falls from his wheelchair. His falls occur as he attempts to transfer onto his bed and toilet. In a few instances he has slid out of his wheelchair and onto the floor; on one occasion his wheelchair tipped over during a transfer.* A.C.*'s medical problems include a stroke with leg weakness and depression for which he takes an antidepressant. Occasionally, he feels dizzy when transferring from his wheelchair.*

Questions

1. With the information you have about this resident, what specific interventions would you include in his care plan in order to decrease the risk of falls from his wheelchair?
2. Based on your care plan, for which outcomes would you monitor this resident?

Case 7

R.E. *is an 89-year-old nursing facility resident with moderate dementia, arthritis of the knees, and polymyalgia rheumatica (i.e., a syndrome affecting older people characterized by proximal joint or muscle pain) for which he takes steroid medication.* He *demonstrates poor bed transfers and ambulation.* R.E. *uses a walker, but the device is unsafe.*

Questions

1. With the information you have about this resident, what specific interventions would you include in his care plan in order to reduce fall risk?
2. Based on your care plan, for which outcomes would you monitor this resident?

Case 8

M.S. *is an 82-year-old hospital patient admitted for falls. She demonstrates poor bed, toilet, and chair transfers, which are the result of lower limb weakness.* M.S.'s *cognition is mildly impaired. She has hypothyroidism and is on replacement therapy.*

Questions

1. With the information you have about this patient, what specific interventions would you include in her care plan in order to improve mobility and reduce fall risk?
2. Based on your care plan, for which outcomes would you monitor this patient?

Case 9

W.M. *is a 79-year-old hospital patient. On the day she was admitted, she slipped in her urine while attempting to toilet.* W.M. *is now afraid to go to the bathroom by herself and has developed a fear of falling and urinary incontinence as a result. She is able to transfer independently and her cognitive abilities are unaffected.*

Questions

1. With the information you have about this patient, what specific intervention would you include in her care plan in order to reduce incontinence and her fear of falling?
2. Based on your care plan, for which outcomes would you monitor this patient?

Case 10

M.M. *is an 82-year-old nursing facility resident who has experienced several falls from bed.* M.M.'s *medical problems consist of* Parkinson's *disease and osteoporosis. She takes no medication. Recently, her nurses found* M.M. *sprawled on the floor by her bed. To prevent further bed falls, she was placed in mechanical restraints.*

Questions

1. With the information you have about this resident, what specific interventions would you include in her care plan to reduce the risk of falls and eliminate the need for mechanical restraints?
2. Based on your care plan, for which outcomes would you monitor this resident?

Answers for Case 1

Question 1

- Primary care provider to evaluate patient's nocturia for reversible causes.
- Primary care provider to evaluate patient's Parkinson's disease and arthritis and her need for Parkinson's and analgesic medications in order to improve ambulation.
- Nursing to provide a night-light in patient's bedroom in order to provide safe ambulation to the bathroom.
- Physical Therapy to evaluate patient for a walker in order to improve ambulation.

- Physical Therapy to evaluate patient and provide an exercise program in order to improve ambulation.

Question 2

- Monitor patient for further falls. If falls occur under similar circumstances, consider a bed alarm system to alert staff when E.L. gets out of bed so that they can offer assistance with ambulation, or provide a bedside commode to eliminate E.L.'s need to travel to the bathroom.
- Monitor symptoms of nocturia (i.e., getting up at night to urinate).
- Monitor patient's ability to ambulate and for safe use of her walker.

Answers for Case 2

Question 1

- Primary care provider to evaluate the dose of diuretic in order to reduce risk of dehydration and orthostatic hypotension.
- Nursing to provide resident with sufficient fluid intake in order to treat dehydration.
- Nursing to request that resident asks for assistance when getting up from bed and to provide assistance with rising from bed in order to reduce risk of falls related to orthostatic hypotension.
- Nursing to check whether resident also experiences orthostatic hypotension with other transfer activities, such as chair and toilet transfers, and provide appropriate modifications as needed in order to support safe transfer activities.

Question 2

- Monitor G.B. for further falls. If falls occur, refer to primary care provider for another evaluation. If falls occur with rising from bed or resident fails to ask for assistance, or both, consider the use of a bed alarm system.
- Monitor G.B.'s blood pressure to ensure that it is controlled, particularly if the dose of diuretics is reduced.
- Monitor fluid intake to avoid the risk of dehydration.

Answers for Case 3

Question 1

- Primary care provider to evaluate resident's worsening cognition and agitation for reversible causes. Consider short-term medication to control agitation, but only if behavior results in harm to self or others.
- Physical Therapy to evaluate resident and provide a walker and an ambulation program in order to support safe ambulation.
- Nursing to provide resident with structured activities in the late afternoon in order to avoid agitation and eliminate need for medication to control agitation.

Question 2

- Monitor for further falls. If falls occur under similar circumstances, consider hip-padding system in order to decrease risk of hip fractures.
- Monitor cognition and agitation.
- Monitor for effectiveness and side effects of medication, if given for agitation.
- Monitor ambulation and for safe use of walker. If resident fails to use her walker, consider a Merry Walker to allow independent ambulation.
- Monitor for sundowning (i.e., late afternoon or early evening confusion).

Answers for Case 4

Question 1

- Primary care provider to evaluate patient's leg weakness for treatable causes.
- Physical Therapy to evaluate patient and provide rehabilitative exercise program to improve his leg strength.
- Nursing to evaluate patient's bed and provide modifications such as low height, half bed side rail for transfer assistance, and nonslip floor surfaces in order to support safe transfers.
- Physical Therapy to evaluate patient's toilet and provide modifications such as grab bars, toilet riser, and nonslip floor surface in order to support safe transfers.

- Nursing to request that patient asks for help with transfers and to provide assistance in order to support safe transfers.

Question 2

- Monitor patient for further falls. If patient falls from bed, fails to ask for assistance, or both, consider bed alarm system to alert staff when patient gets out of bed.
- Monitor for effectiveness of bed and toilet modifications.
- Monitor for effectiveness of rehabilitative exercise program.

Answers for Case 5

Question 1

- Primary care provider to evaluate the causes of the patient's falls and risk factors for further falls (i.e., to examine for treatable causes and modifiable risk factors).
- Physical Therapy to evaluate patient and provide an exercise program in order to improve L.R.'s balance and reduce her fear of falling.
- Nursing to provide assistance with patient's transfers and ambulation in order to support safe activities and reduce her fear of falling.

Question 2

- Home Care to provide patient with a personal emergency response system in order to reduce the risk of extensive lie times.
- Home Care Physical Therapy to continue exercise program, if needed.
- Home Care Occupational Therapy to evaluate the safety of L.R.'s home environment; modify kitchen/closet shelves in order to reduce risk of balance loss and provide bathtub equipment in order to support safe tub transfers.

Answers for Case 6

Question 1

- Primary care provider to evaluate resident's depression and antidepressant dosage for medication side effects and possible decreased medication dose or selection of an alternative drug.

- Physical Therapy to teach resident safe wheelchair transfer techniques, provide an exercise program to strengthen his legs, modify resident's wheelchair (e.g., brakes, seat height, anti-tipping device to support safe transfers), and provide toilet grab bars and half bed side rail to support safe toilet and bed transfers.
- Nursing to provide resident with a nonslip wheelchair seat cushion in order to prevent him from sliding out of his wheelchair.

Question 2

- Monitor for further falls from the wheelchair. If falls occur, reevaluate wheelchair interventions.
- Monitor depression and effectiveness/side effects of medication.
- Monitor for effectiveness of Physical Therapy and Nursing interventions.

Answers for Case 7

Question 1

- Primary care provider to evaluate resident's steroid medication for necessity or for tapering off of the dosage.
- Nursing to evaluate resident's bed and provide modifications, such as lower height and half bed side rails, for transfer assistance to support safe transfers.
- Physical Therapy to evaluate resident's walker and the need for an exercise program in order to improve leg strength and ambulation.

Question 2

- Monitor for further falls from bed.
- Monitor bed transfers and for effectiveness of bed modifications.
- Monitor ambulation and for safe use of the walker.

Answers for Case 8

Question 1

- Primary care provider to evaluate patient's leg weakness and altered cognition for treatable causes.

- Nursing to evaluate patient's bed and provide modifications in order to support safe transfers.
- Physical Therapy to evaluate patient and provide an exercise program in order to improve transfers. Physical Therapy to evaluate and provide chair and toilet modifications in order to support safe transfers.

Question 2

- Monitor for further falls.
- Monitor thyroid status and for effectiveness of replacement therapy.
- Monitor cognition.
- Monitor transfers.
- Monitor for effectiveness of chair and toilet modifications.

Answers for Case 9

Question 1

- Nursing to provide patient with a bedside commode to eliminate the need for traveling to the bathroom and to reduce incontinence.
- Nursing to provide assistance with toileting, as needed.
- Nonslip strips of a noncontrasting color to be applied to patient's bathroom floor in the event that patient resumes bathroom activity.

Question 2

- Monitor for incontinence.
- Monitor for fear of falling.
- Monitor for effectiveness of bedside commode.

Answers for Case 10

Question 1

- Primary care provider to evaluate resident's Parkinson's disease for the need for medication.
- Nursing to evaluate resident's bed and provide modifications in order to support safe bed transfers. Mechanical restraints to be removed from the resident. If the resident continues to fall, consider the use of a bed alarm system.

- Nursing to evaluate resident's need for low-height bed to reduce the risk of injurious falls from bed. Provide bed, if necessary.

Question 2

- Monitor for further falls from bed.
- Monitor Parkinson's disease and for effectiveness of medications, if given.
- Monitor for effectiveness of bed alarm system, if used.
- Monitor for effectiveness of low-height bed, if used.

Index

Page numbers followed by "f" indicate figures, page numbers followed by "t" indicate tables, page numbers followed by "n" indicate an endnote.